Holding God's Hand
through the Storms *of* Life

Trekking Through Worries &
Problems to Find Joy & Peace

Nancy L. Harry

Copyright © 2015 by Nancy L. Harry

Holding God's Hand Through the Storms of Life
Trekking Through Worries & Problems to Find Joy & Peace
by Nancy L. Harry

Printed in the United States of America.

ISBN 9781628391503

All rights reserved solely by the author. The author guarantees all contents are original and do not infringe upon the legal rights of any other person or work. No part of this book may be reproduced in any form without the permission of the author. The views expressed in this book are not necessarily those of the publisher.

Unless otherwise indicated, Bible quotations are taken from the Holy Bible, New International Version®, NIV® of the Bible. Copyright © 1973, 1978, 1984, 2011 by Biblica, Inc.®. Used by permission. All rights reserved worldwide.

Scriptured quotations identified TLB are from The Living Bible copyright © 1971 by Tyndale House Foundation. Used by permission of Tyndale House Publishers Inc., Carol Stream, Illinois 60188. All rights reserved.

Scriptured quotations identified NLT are from the New Living Translation copyright © 1996, 2004, 2007, 2013 by Tyndale House Foundation. Used by permission of Tyndale House Publishers Inc., Carol Stream, Illinois 60188. All rights reserved.

www.xulonpress.com

Table of Contents

Introduction vii

PART 1 Through the Worries

Chapter 1 :   What to Do?............................11

Chapter 2 :   Fear Is Born................................27

Chapter 3 :   Sink or Float.............................37

Chapter 4 :   A Balancing Act........................53

PART 2 : Over the Bumps

Chapter 5 :   Twists and Turns 65

Chapter 6 :   A Pity Party...............................87

Chapter 7 :   Wounds of the Heart 103

Chapter 8 :   Bemoaning the Times...................117

PART 3 : Peace Found at Last

Chapter 9 :   Opportunities...........................129

Chapter 10 : Comforting Prayer 143

Chapter 11 : New Memories 153

Chapter 12 : Blessing of Peace.........................165

End Notes 181

Further Reading. 185

About the Author. 187

Introduction

"Come to me, all you who are weary and burdened, and I will give you rest." Matthew 11:28

In your hands, you hold a book that shines a beacon of light on the contradiction and struggle that exists between your faith in God and your many worries, doubts and fears. The ability to worry, doubt and fear comes along with your emotional make-up. Worry can help you care about or be concerned for others. Doubt can cause you to avoid making mistakes. Fear can prevent you from doing foolish things. Yet, if these particular emotions become extreme they cross the line of beneficial. May the suggestions offered here help you walk that balanced line, as you learn to rely more and more on God.

The storms of life bring unwanted and hurtful experiences into your life. You will find ways to handle the negative words or actions absorbed deep in the heart. Learn how to put to rest the hurts and wounds that want to linger instead of heal. Discover and embrace a greater closeness with God as you walk through the many troubles that work their way into your life. Experience a joy and peace in your soul that comes only from a caring, loving God, in spite of problems that stop by now and then.

Get ready to explore how walking hand in hand with an amazing God can make a difference in your life. May each story, illustration and example bring encouragement and more truth to help you enjoy your life to the fullest.

> "May God our Father
> and the Lord Jesus Christ
> give you all of his blessings,
> and great peace of heart and mind."
> 1 Corinthians 1:3 (TLB)

PART 1

Through the Worries

Put everything in God's hand,
then God's hand will be in everything.

Chapter 1

What to Do?

An unseen event brought traffic to a complete stop. Impatient drivers wait in their idling cars. In the midst of this bumper-to-bumper traffic, I find myself in the center of the bridge that stretches across the Susquehanna River.

Finally! We are moving again. I step on the gas. Oh no, my car stopped running! I turn the key, but the engine won't start. What is wrong with my car? Was it overheating? The cars slowly creep past on my right. Those behind me continue to be patient. Are the worries settling in? Yes they are!

"Oh Lord," I pray, "What am I going to do? I'm in the middle of a bridge in the passing lane and my car won't budge. Help me!" Within minutes, a large flatbed truck pulls up beside me with two unknown men sitting in the high cab. They signal to me.

"Do you need help?" one calls out the window.

"No" quickly rolls off my tongue.

Why did I say that? Of course I need help, but I don't know these men. Can I trust them? The traffic ahead of me creeps slowly on, while I hold up the string of oncoming cars behind me. The truck moves a few feet forward and stops. Now he holds up the traffic behind him in the right lane. The cars ahead of him move on. My car still won't start. I am definitely in a full-blown worry mode right now. A knot tightens in my stomach. What am I going to do? "God, help me!"

Again, the man in the truck waves and says, "We can help you. We'll put your car on the back of our truck."

"I'll be all right." Praying again, I said, "Oh God, what am I going to do?" as the traffic in front of me moves farther ahead.

"This is the last time I am offering to help you. Do you want us to help you or not?" the man says, as he leans out the truck's window once more.

"Thank you, Lord, and protect me," I pray under my breath. "Yes, I can use your help. Thank you."

The truck maneuvers into the lane in front of me. My over-heated, unmoving car is pulled onto the back of their truck. I squeeze into the cab of the truck. These two caring men reveal they pick up cars that are being repossessed. These God-sent men dropped me and my ailing car off at a garage on the other side of the river.

God heard my prayer and knew my need even before I did. I'm glad He sent patient men who didn't leave me stranded after my first negative reply. How often do we fail to respond to those first promptings of God in our lives? Are we thankful that He is so patient with us?

Worry and Concern

Worry. What is worry? It is to be or cause to be anxious or uneasy, especially about something uncertain or potentially dangerous. It means something is interfering with your peace of mind causing care, anxiety or apprehension. Concern means something that is of interest or importance to you is affecting, troubling or worrying you or causing you to feel disquiet. Concern is also identified as worry, anxiety or showing concern for someone in trouble. Worry, care and concern are synonyms and are interchangeable. They imply an uneasy and burdened state of mind.

Many things cause us to worry or be concerned. Worry is a way we show concern for someone in trouble. God had concern for the Israelites, because He cared about them. In His Word we read, "God heard their groaning and he remembered his covenant with Abraham, with Isaac and with Jacob. So God looked on the Israelites and was concerned about them" Exodus 2:24-25. God does not change. His concern for all those that love Him does not change. It causes Him to hear our requests and petitions, and send His angels on our behalf. Because He cares, He is concerned about what transpires in our lives.

If we had no worries, no cares, no concern for others, there would be no love. For example, if someone is doing something dangerous, we tend to worry or be concerned he might get hurt. We may worry that a path a friend is following will lead to unhappiness. When friends or loved ones go off to war, we worry. We want assurance they will come home safely. If a person has a pain in his body, it is the worry or concern that something is wrong that leads him to seek healing.

Worry or fear can be a restraint from doing something foolish, like jumping out a window hoping to fly like a bird. If a person did not have feelings of worry or fear that he might hurt or even kill himself, he might go ahead and do it on a whim. Unfortunately, we have heard of small children who have not developed these restraints, doing this very thing.

Paul felt the stress of being concerned or worried about the new and growing churches. He wrote: "I have the constant worry of how the churches are getting along" 2 Corinthians 11:28 (TLB). He also wrote about his fears: "When we arrived in Macedonia there was no rest for us; outside, trouble was on every hand and all around us; within us, our hearts were full of dread and fear" 2 Corinthians 7:5 (TLB).

Our Priorities

Jesus said, "Therefore I tell you, do not worry about your life, what you will eat or drink; or about your body, what you will wear. Is not life more important than food, and the body more than clothes?" Matthew 6:25. In this Scripture, He urges us to think about our priorities. He was not saying we shouldn't consider eating healthy or dressing appropriately.

In verse 31 He said, "So do not worry, saying, 'What shall we eat?' or 'What shall we drink?' or 'What shall we wear?'" He went on to explain, "your heavenly Father knows that you need them. But seek first his kingdom and his righteousness, and all these things will be given to you as well" Matthew 6:32-33. In these Scriptures, Jesus made comparisons between His kingdom and our daily needs. In the Lord's Prayer it says, "your kingdom come, your will be done, on earth as it is in heaven. Give us today our daily bread" Matthew 6:10-11. Although our daily needs are important, He wants us to know His kingdom is much more important and that He is very capable of providing the necessities of life for us.

This makes me think of the Israelites forty year trip through the desert. A trip necessary to prepare them to enter the land they were promised. During those years, God provided their daily food. In the mornings manna rained down from heaven for their bread and in the evenings quails were provided for their meat. He provided water if another natural source was not available, like the time He caused water to burst forth from a rock. During those years, even their shoes did not wear out. Is God able to provide? A definite yes!

These particular verses stress that our *first* priority is to seek the spiritual benefits of His kingdom, rather than the material goods of this world. Goodness, righteousness, mercy, grace, blessings and favor know no bounds in His kingdom. When we put God's way first, He'll see that our physical needs are met as well. Paul described God's kingdom this way, "For the kingdom of God is not a matter of eating and drinking, but of righteousness, peace and joy in the Holy Spirit" Romans 14:17. His kingdom includes His way of doing things. It is one of stability and calm. Many people are oblivious about His kingdom, yet it waits for them. God calls us to come and experience His kingdom. As we move into it, we find His light shines bright, His will is done and our needs are met. It is where all is well and where He dwells.

Jesus asked a thought provoking question, "Can any one of you by worrying add a single hour to your life?" Life is in Jesus. Accepting Him as your Savior by realizing He took the punishment for your sins, releases you to live a life of righteousness, and results in eternal life with a loving God. Your life is in His hands. Worrying is not able to increase your days. God cares about everything that happens in your life. You are very valuable to Him. He desires to take care of you, just as you want to take care of your children. Appreciating His great love makes it easy for Him to take top priority in your life.

Too Much Worry

Our emotions can be beneficial at times, but they can also be misappropriated. It is when the emotions God created in us are misused that they cause trouble. If they become excessive or unfounded, they move from the realm of beneficial to that of harmful. If not kept in check, worry or concern often interferes with our peace of mind and may lead to anxiety and apprehension. Someone who is overly anxious about something cannot relax and enjoy life. The WebMD article on anxiety says:

"Feeling worried or nervous is a normal part of everyday life. Everyone frets or feels anxious from time to time. Mild to moderate anxiety can help you focus your attention, energy, and motivation. If anxiety is severe, you may have feelings of helplessness, confusion, and extreme worry that are out of proportion with the actual seriousness or likelihood of the feared event. Overwhelming anxiety that interferes with daily life is not normal."[1]

I have been guilty of worrying about the future and guilty of being too preoccupied with the past. This made it almost impossible for me to enjoy the present. Does unproductive and unconstructive worry fill your thoughts so much that you never enjoy a moment's peace? Do those thoughts keep you so preoccupied that you do not have time to plan, set goals or have a vision for the life you still have to live? It is hard to remain at peace once worry clutters the mind. How can a person be full of worry and happy at the same time?

When we worry excessively, we are not putting our trust in God. Yet, He offers us both life and peace. What marvelous promises. Paul advised, "Do not be anxious about anything, but in every situation, by prayer and petition, with thanksgiving, present your requests to God" Philippians 4:6. "Every situation" includes the big and the little things of life. If it is important enough to worry about or become anxious over, then it is important enough to pray about it.

Worry does not solve problems or solve the possibility of future problems, action does. Instead of letting your worries and concerns keep you anxious or upset, let them bring you to God's doorstep. Through prayer, He can intervene and by His acts of kindness toward you, show you His love. He is capable of handling situations in a way that will be in your best interest.

Big and Little Things

Do you forget to pray about those little matters that come up in your life? Maybe you think they are too insignificant to bother God with them. Yet, they continue to take over your thoughts and emotions. On the other hand, it could be that it never occurred to you to pray about them.

I used to have horrible nightmares, which caused me to wake up screaming. It would frighten my family members and wake them from their sleep. I thought it was just one of those things I had to live with. It never occurred to me to talk to God about it. One day I overheard a person telling her friend that she used to have very bad nightmares. She prayed about them and they soon went away. What a revelation that was to me. I began to realize I could talk to Him about anything that upset or bothered me. I was quickly learning that He could change or fix what I couldn't.

Sometimes it takes patience to wait for an answer from the Lord. We have to spend time in God's waiting room. Although some answers come more quickly than others do,

His schedule does not always correspond with ours. The writer of this Psalm also put patience into practice in his life; "I wait for the Lord, my whole being waits, and in his word I put my hope" Psalm 130:5. Did you notice that this writer put his hope in God's Word? I heard author and speaker Bob Hazlett say, "Worry is imagining the worst and hope is imagining the best." How true.

Instead of feeling anxious or full of worry, take your concerns and requests to the Lord. Then, be sure to thank Him for His answers. You will soon notice: "And the peace of God, which transcends all understanding, will guard your hearts and your minds in Christ Jesus" Philippians 4:7. What a relief it is to experience the inner tranquility that comes from no longer worrying—about your worries.

Swinging

Human nature may send us swinging—swinging back and forth like a pendulum or from one extreme to another. So be careful not to go to extremes and put yourself in harmful situations or take a flippant attitude while saying, "Nothing bothers me" or "I'm not worried or "I trust God." Look at the following example from the life of Jesus as He was tempted by the devil to jump from a building to prove who He was:

> "Then the devil took him to the holy city and had him stand on the highest point of the temple. "If you are the Son of God," he said, "throw yourself down. For it is written:
> "'He will command his angels concerning you, and they will lift you up in their hands, so

that you will not strike your foot against a stone.'" Jesus answered him, "It is also written: 'Do not put the Lord your God to the test.'" Matthew 4:5-8

Jesus could have said, "I'm not worried. God will protect me, so I'll prove who I am and jump from this building." However, He did not respond in that way. God does not want us to act foolish, irrationally or irresponsibly.

What worry is not: it is not a means of controlling our situations. Instead, it is feeling distressed, troubled or anxious about something, someone or future events. The worry that doesn't motivate you to do something about the problem or to seek an answer, keeps you busy without being productive. Corrie Ten Boom said, "Worrying does not empty tomorrow of its troubles. It empties today of its strength." So let's press forward through the challenges to a better tomorrow.

Express Feelings

Life does not come problem-free or trouble-free. Most of us do not dwell in a life of ease. It would be wonderful if we could live without problems, but the reality is that they are part of this life. Some people think if they accept Jesus and become a Christian, they won't have any more problems. However, becoming a Christian does not mean that magically problems and heartaches vanish.

Jesus said we would have trouble in this world. He was upfront and truthful with us. He warned us, not wanting us to be caught by surprise. He said, "I have told you these things, so that in me you may have peace. In this world you will have trouble. But take heart! I have overcome the world"

John 16:33. The Apostle Paul warned the disciples to remain true to the faith, even though their lives wouldn't be easy. At the same time, he prepared and encouraged them by saying, "We must go through many hardships to enter the kingdom of God" Acts 14:22.

James, the half-brother of Jesus, told us the best place to start if adverse situations arise. He said, "Is anyone among you in trouble? Let them pray" James 5:13. Instead of worrying about a problem that is perceived as unsolvable or as a possible problem in the future, turn the focus to praying for an answer and look for solutions. In other words, handle worry by praying about the situation. I find spending time with the Lord relieves the pressure and constant worry.

Think of problems as challenges that need solved before they become overwhelming and drag you down. God, in His infinite wisdom, didn't leave us without help. Jesus asked the Father to send us another Counselor, who is the Comforter and the Spirit of truth. In answer to this request, our heavenly Father sent the Holy Spirit to earth to reside in those who would accept Jesus Christ as their Savior. The Holy Spirit will lead and guide us, and give us the wisdom to find the right solutions. Ask Him for His help.

Would it be better to pretend you don't have a problem or worries when you do? This is not a good idea. Repressed feelings are not healthy. Imagine blowing up a balloon. If you keep stuffing it with air, it will eventually burst! The same thing could happen to you. If you keep stuffing and holding your feelings in for too long, you will eventually explode too. It may not always come as anger; it could come in the form of sickness or depression. Bottled up emotions tend to come back stronger than ever, since you are not really dealing with them. Therefore, it is never to your advantage to repress negative feelings, whether they come from hurt or anger. The shortest verse in the Bible says, "Jesus wept." Hurt, pain, grief need expressed.

Of course, it is important to express feelings and emotions in an appropriate manner. One way is to write down the things that have hurt you, that are a struggle or have saddened you. As difficult times swept through my life, I wrote in a journal to help relieve the negative thoughts and feelings that came with those times. It is best to talk about them, but even writing those things down can be helpful.

Talk with a trusted friend, family member or counselor. When choosing someone to talk with, consider this word of caution: some people are not good listeners and some do not have your best interests in mind. So be careful who you trust with your heart. If it is possible to work things through with the offending party, that is even better.

Even more important than going to others is to go to the Lord. Never leave Him out. Run to the throne before you run to the phone. Instead of letting negative emotions control you, give them away—not through vented rage, violence or anger toward others, but to the Lord. He is always waiting to listen. He is the One who has the ability to help you with the problems that life throws your way. Peter encourages you to "Let him have all your worries and cares, for he is always thinking about you and watching everything that concerns you" 1 Peter 5:7 (TLB).

Years ago I was a supervisor for a home party plan company. Unbeknown to me, one of the women I trained was having trouble doing the paperwork after holding a show. Receiving a call from the company to advise me of the situation, I gave her a call. I asked her why she didn't call me when she found it difficult to fill out the forms. She said she called her sister who helped her. Her sister was not with the company and had no training, so the forms were filled out incorrectly. How often do we go to others for answers and are reluctant to ask God for His help, when He is the One who has the answers we need? I heard the Lord say,

> "I am a loving God. But I will not endure evil forever. The time for justice will come. I long and desire for you to know me. You turn to this one and you turn to that one. Why do you not turn to me? Don't you know how much I want to help you? I want to turn the tide in your life, lift you up and set you on your feet. I love you so. If you would only turn to me, I will make myself known to you. Then you will be my sons and daughters and I will be your God."

Releasing Our Burdens

Some of us like doing everything ourselves. We want to feel like we are in control of every situation we find ourselves in. This makes it difficult to rely on the Lord and allow Him to help with those worries and problems.

Maybe you find yourself discussing your problems with God, yet at the same time, still trying to fix everything by yourself. The following suggestions may aid with learning to put your confidence and trust in Him during difficult life situations:

> ➤ Picture yourself throwing your problem in the waste can. Well, some of us do go back to the waste can

and retrieve something we decided not to throw away after all. Sometimes this is what we do with our problems too. So picture the garbage truck carrying it away.
➢ When I was a young child, my father played a simple game with me. He made a tight fist and then challenged me to pry his fingers open. It was an impossible task even though I struggled with all my might. Envision putting your worries and problems into the open hand of God and watching Him close His eternal hand around them. Now you can't take them back without prying open the fingers of God, and I would venture to say that would also be impossible.
➢ A speaker I heard at a seminar was also an avid basketball player. She envisions putting her concerns inside a basketball and bouncing them up to God.
➢ At a conference, we took a brick for each hurt and carried it around with us all day. The inconvenience and weight of the bricks grew heavier as the day went on. Like these bricks, our hurts and disappointments weigh us down and get in our way of doing things that are more profitable. At the end of the day, we laid the bricks and all they represented before the Lord.

The nature of your concern doesn't matter, whether financial, business, or personal. Let God in on the situation whatever it is. Ask Him to do what is best for you in each particular situation. Jesus prayed to the Father, "Yet not as I will, but as you will" Matthew 26:39. At times, what you want, expect or hope for is not what God had in mind. Do you desire what you think is the best solution or His solution?

He is aware of much more than we are. He sees the whole picture. It takes a great weight off our shoulders as we learn to depend and rely on Him in every situation. Knowing that all we see is His and that He is great and powerful, yet full of love for us, "Let us then approach God's throne of grace with confidence, so that we may receive mercy and find grace to help us in our time of need" Hebrews 4:16.

It is all right to continue to talk with God about things you already discussed with Him, especially when they keep bothering you or it is still unclear which direction to take. Jesus said, "So I say to you: Ask and it will be given to you; seek and you will find; knock and the door will be opened to you" Luke 11:9. Seeking and knocking requires effort; it is not necessarily a one-time thing. Jesus urges boldness and even persistence when approaching God.

Along with your prayers to seek His help and direction, it might be helpful to further your knowledge in those areas as well. Also, take time to study His Word on specific topics that concern you for additional direction and wisdom. Psalm 119:105 says, "Your word is a lamp for my feet, a light on my path."

As hurtful memories rise up to bother you, stop them in their tracks by talking back to them. For example, tell those thoughts: "I already gave this situation to God; I already forgave this person; I'm not going to dwell on this anymore." Talking back to negative thoughts keeps them from getting a grip and ruining your day. Most of the hurtful times that continue to replay in my mind seem to come at night and interfere with the sleep I need. I give the memories an opportunity to pass through, not stay. Then I move on to pray for a while. I find playing soothing music, especially praise music helps too.

Unfortunately, traveling back in time to redo the past is not an option. While it could help to analyze your past to work out issues, keep in mind it is no longer a part of your present. Now it is time to move on to a better tomorrow.

Moving Forward

Some people feel they are doing something productive when they worry. It is their way of paying attention to the problem. But can a person really change anything by worrying? A church sign I saw along the road said, "Worry is the misuse of the imagination."

Since we don't know what the future holds, it's not helpful to get caught up in worrying about it. It just uses up our time. Matthew 6:34 tells us not to "worry about tomorrow, for tomorrow will worry about itself. Each day has enough trouble of its own." Your job is to take care of today. Do the best you can right now. Every day is a new opportunity to make new memories. Robert J. Hastings wrote, "It isn't the burdens of today that drive men mad. Rather, it is regret over yesterday or fear of tomorrow. Regret and fear are twin thieves who would rob us of today."[2]

Begin setting good plans and goals for your future, leaving excessive worry and fear out. It is more beneficial to look forward with optimism and a sense of excitement for all God is going to do. It is time to think forward not backward. Thinking ahead tends to move us forward. Thinking about the past tends to hold us back. It brings us to a standstill and puts our futures on hold. Holding onto the past is not going to change it.

When you stop living in the past and stop worrying about the future, it frees you to live in the present. God cares about you as an individual. He cares about what is happening in your life. He wants to bless you now. He loves you now. Realizing how much He cares is enough to fill you with joy. At a conference, I heard evangelist and author Patricia King say, "Worry just attracts more worry. If you are going to go through a trial, you might as well go through it happy."

The quest is to live in God's peace, leaning on Him to help you with the problems and troubles that come your way. He expects you to do what you can and trust Him with the rest. Check to see who your trust is in. Is it in God, yourself or someone else? Remind the worries that you trust God. It is time to let the past go and move forward without the worries and fears. So remember: the past is over, the future has not arrived and today is a new day. Dr. James O. Davis, founder of Cutting Edge International, said it this way: "We need to unhook from yesterday. Learn to enjoy today. And, don't borrow from tomorrow's problems."

Chapter 2

Fear Is Born

Evening has finally arrived and I am ready to relax. I rushed throughout the day to get as many things checked off my to-do list as I could. The rushing and accomplishments of the day took its toll on my mind and body.

Settling into my favorite chair, I turn on the television to the news channel's ongoing dialogue. I see reports about a death, a beating, a robbery, a fire and on it goes. I decide— no more television news for me. I pick up the newspaper. As I read, my mind is bombarded with more in-depth details of the destructive happenings of the week. I decide—no more reading newspapers for me. I choose a movie to calm my mind. I just want to vegetate for a while. I want to unwind and relax. The movie is sprinkled with sexual put-downs and violence. Oh, I feel a headache coming on. Is there no end to this madness?

Soon I'm afraid to say hi to a neighbor, afraid to walk down the street and afraid to let my children leave the house. God knows His world has gone topsy-turvy and is filled with crime and hatred. He looks for His love, His mercy and His compassion among the people. Who will He find doing His will when He returns?

Was it safer when I was a child? Was it less worrisome? I remember watching a monster movie one evening as my brother, sister and I gathered close together. We felt safer and less frightened huddled in each other's presence. Later that night, as I snuggled under my bedcovers, dark shadows and the thoughts of hiding monsters kept my eyes wide-awake.

"Go to sleep," Dad called from somewhere below.

"Oh, if I could only sleep," I thought. A question soon invaded my longing to sleep, "What is that dark shadow at the bottom of my bed?"

I gathered my courage. With a giant leap, I jumped from my bed, slid down the stairs and flung my little body into the arms of my bewildered mother. Up the stairs we went, hand in hand. A pile of clothes lay jumbled at the end of the bed. I vowed to never pile clothes on the bottom of my bed again.

Goodbye to Fear

Our worries may come from fears or grow into fears. Childhood fears spill over into today. The terrible news on the television, radio or internet instills worries and fears. They may come from what we read in the newspapers or magazines. Shocking experiences leave us full of fears. Some people even live in a continual state of fear.

Fear could also be wrong believing, a negative thought that can literally attract what you fear the most. Job expressed it this way, "What I feared has come upon me; what I dreaded has happened to me" Job 3:25. Sometimes you are not conscious of your harmful or fearful thoughts. You could even have undesirable thoughts about yourself that you don't realize. Jeremiah 17:9 says, "The heart is deceitful above all things and beyond cure. Who can understand it?" Begin to analyze your thoughts to weed those peace stealers out. Hanging onto these types of thoughts and beliefs can affect your quality of life by keeping around negative situations. For instance, people who fear rejection project "I know you won't like me," then find themselves rejected. Those who believe they are weak and incapable project neediness. People who want rescued project this need and draw controllers, those who like to dominate. Only this scenario eventually leads to resentment in the one being controlled. If the weak one grows or acts stronger, it upsets the denominator; the controller doesn't like losing his position. The adverse results from these examples lead to codependent relationships and victim mentalities. With Christ, you are not weak but strong. You are very important to God. He doesn't reject you, but accepts and loves you.

President Franklin D. Roosevelt said, "The only thing we have to fear is fear itself," during his first inaugural address in 1933. If fear tries to come over you, remind yourself that God has not given you a spirit of fear, but a spirit of power and love. He lovingly says,

> "So do not fear, for I am with you;
> do not be dismayed, for I am your God.
> I will strengthen you and help you;
> I will uphold you with my righteous right hand."
> Isaiah 41:10

In the face of fear, He is able to comfort your heart and give you unusual courage and peace. His heart cries to your heart to follow Him. He loves you with an everlasting love. See Him as the God who loves you. Drink in His love letting it fill you. I am so thankful He is the center of my life. I often wonder how I would survive if He wasn't there to lean on and talk to. I absorb His love and His strength daily.

Fear that runs rampant will interfere with your enjoyment of life. Begin now to replace fear with faith and trust in God. He is not the author of unfounded fears. He does not want you living in this kind of fear. Run to Him, hold His hand and go for the victory, washing away those troublesome fears!

Hidden Fear

As I contemplated the question, "What does God want removed from my life?" the word *fear* came to mind. My first reaction was surprise. I assumed I didn't have any fears. Almost immediately from somewhere within, I heard the word *fear* once again. This time I asked the Lord to show me if I had any fears that needed to be removed.

The diagnosis of colon cancer had led to two major surgeries, followed by a season of recovery while enduring the side effects of chemotherapy. The treatment had drained my energy, sapped my memory, destroyed my immune system and made me feel very vulnerable. It is not something I wish to repeat. Did I fear it? No, so I thought. Yet every time I had a pain in my body, somewhere deep inside, a dark question arose asking me if it could be coming back. A fear had grown out of that experience.

The thought of death, a cessation of this life, causes great fear for many people. There is the unknown of what awaits them if anything, the loss of the life, the loss of family and friends they have known, and the possibility of pain and suffering. "What if I should die?" I asked myself. As a believer in Jesus Christ as my Savior, my soul will go where He is—to heaven where He resides. After the death of this physical body, my next moments of consciousness will lead me into the loving presence of my Savior and my God. What can be better than that?

What fears do you have? Let God reveal them to you. Then follow the leading of the Holy Spirit to deal with them in the best ways for you.

Reaction to Danger

Occasionally fear can be more than a feeling of excessive worry or doubt, but one of uneasiness or apprehension. It can result from a reaction to the presence or nearness of danger or evil. The body has a built-in warning system meant to warn you of danger and that is a good thing. Sometimes it could even be the Holy Spirit warning you of immediate danger.

My mother found herself in such a situation. She had arrived home from running some errands. As she entered her home and moved about, a sense of fear came over her. She decided to leave and come back later. It was confirmed. Her home had been burglarized. Responding to her sensation of fear by leaving again, may have saved her from bodily harm by the intruder.

Controlling Fear

Fear can cause an inability to move forward or cause a person to become ineffective or powerless. Controlling fear hinders the ability to be resourceful and holds us back from finding a solution. It is important to find that place where we feel calm, so ideas and the next step become clear. It is not possible to be creative when we are full of panic or under stress. Science says fear causes the rational parts of the brain to shut down. This makes us feel like IQ points are lost.

Fears can also turn into anxiety attacks. In these situations, a person may need the benefit of counseling and/or medication to get this type of anxiety under control. An anxiety disorder referred to as GAD is an exaggerated or unfounded general state of worry and anxiety about events, activities or individual concerns. This type of anxiety interferes with a person's daily life. Other symptoms are also associated with it. People with this disorder suffer from constant worry and tension that is much worse than the anxiety most people experience occasionally. As with major clinical depression, a person can't just snap out of this serious condition. For people diagnosed with GAD or clinical depression, it is very important for them to continue working with their doctor.

God continues to ask us to rest in Him and to trust Him to help us with all the various situations that come into our lives. David said, "Whoever dwells in the shelter of the Most High will rest in the shadow of the Almighty. I will say of the Lord, 'He is my refuge and my fortress, my God, in whom I trust'" Psalm 91:1-2.

Fear No Man

> "Fear of man will prove to be a snare,
> but whoever trusts in the LORD is kept safe."
> Proverbs 29:25

Do you fear the anger or the hurtful and negative words of others? Are you afraid they will not love you or accept you? Do you fear their rejection? Ask yourself, "Does it really matter in the overall scheme of things?" Sharing something I was concerned about with my daughter, she asked, "Will it really matter five years from now or ten years from now?"

The people whose acceptance we crave are just like us. They want love and acceptance, too. They do not care for rejection either. God asks us to love others because that is His way. However, people are fickle; they can love you one day and the next day become your enemy.

You do not have to do anything wrong for people to be jealous of you, lie about you or betray you. They may use you as their scapegoat, eliminating their need to take responsibility for their own sins and wrongdoing. Jesus was an example of this truth. He knows and understands the hurt you often suffer through no fault of your own. Scripture tells us this about Jesus: "But first he must suffer many things and be rejected by this generation" Luke 17:25. Judas, His ministry treasurer and disciple, betrayed him. He was rejected by His closest friends and disciples when He was about to lose His very life. Despised and rejected by others, He definitely knows what it is like. He relates. He gets it.

One time I asked the Lord, "Why do I keep having so many bad experiences?" Maybe some of you have had the same question. Then I asked Him to show me if there was something I was doing that caused these troublesome situations in my life. He reminded me that He had also been betrayed, lied about, lied to, and beaten. At times, He was ignored and unappreciated. He endured loss. He encountered the gamut of emotional, physical and verbal abuse in His lifetime. Then He said, "Now you are just like me." I thought, "If the sinless Christ endured suffering, why did I think I wouldn't?"

Even though Jesus suffered greatly, He didn't continue to dwell on those negative events that took place in His life, as we often do. He remembered who He was—the Son of God. He remembered His heavenly Father loved Him. He came to us with a purpose and focused on it. Fulfilling His purpose He qualified to become our High Priest and received a name above all names.

Remember who you are—a daughter or son of the living God. Remember you are loved by your heavenly Father. Paul said, "You are not your own; you were bought at a price" 1 Corinthians 6:19-20. You were bought with the lifeblood of God's Son, so He is not planning on leaving you or forsaking you. He has a purpose for your life, with plans to give you hope and a future.

It is in our best interest to fear God our maker. Men can temporarily break our hearts or harm our bodies, but God decides whether we live forever in His presence or in outer darkness. How He feels about us should be more important to us than what other people may think. Ask yourself, "Why fear someone who eventually dies and whose memory eventually disappears?" Owen Strachan, assistant professor of Christian theology at Boyce College in Louisville, Kentucky said, "If you fear man, God will become small to you. The approval of fellow sinners will matter more to you, than obeying God by the witness of his Word."

God's justice, mercy and love last forever. So why live in fear of people's oppression or fear their anger all day long? David depended on the Lord and knew He was actively involved in his life. He was rejoicing as he said, "The Lord is my light and my salvation—whom shall I fear? The Lord is the stronghold of my life—of whom shall I be afraid?" Psalm 27:1. It is true that God's mercies are new every day. Walk in the confidence of His acceptance and His love. It is time to enjoy the life He came to give you and intended for you to have.

Fear of the Lord

Many Scriptures talk about the "fear of the Lord." The Hebrew or Greek translated *fear* means reverent, reverence or to hold in awe when used in reference to the Lord. Revere means to fear out of respect or to show devoted honor. Similar words are worship, adore and venerate. As we honor and reverence the Lord, the benefits of true knowledge and wisdom follow.

God is our ultimate judge, but even more, He is a God who loves us. He is holy, good and righteous. Because of these characteristics, He does not approve of sin. He knows sin only brings sorrow, pain and death in the end. We would not choose those results for our family and friends either. "If anyone respects and fears God, he will hate evil. For wisdom hates pride, arrogance, corruption, and deceit of every kind" Proverbs 8:13 (TLB).

Other people may temporarily bring a smile to our faces or a moment of joy into our lives. However, the everlasting joy and gladness we know when God forgives us doesn't even begin to compare. Jesus, our redeemer, is the One who came to save us. He paid the price for our sins and wiped our slate clean. He is the wonderful Messiah, the Christ, and our Savior.

God not only made us, He created the universe. He is the One who spread out the stars and made the earth. He is out of our league; there is no comparison. This is the greatness of an eternal God, who longs to comfort you and fill you with joy. It doesn't matter what the situation is; He is there with you. He wants you to live the best life you can—here and now. As you live a life in honor and reverence to Him, speak what He says, believe for His best and expect your circumstances to line up with His Word. May peace, love and faith reign in your life every day.

Chapter 3

Sink or Float

As I relax and look out over the lake, the ripples slap against the bank. I try to visualize Jesus walking on the water. I watch the boats filled with people come in and out from the landing, floating on the watery glass, never sinking into the dark blue water. A lone black duck floats among the reeds. I recall watching a video of a little lizard running across the top of a pond. I didn't even know they could do that. The little lizard didn't sink either.

Boats and ships float. Ducks float. Jesus, you might say, floated on His feet. For a few moments, Peter did too. See Matthew 14:25-29. Even the little lizard ran on top of the water. I wondered—why do we sink? However, my son had a friend who was extremely buoyant. While doing the back float in our pool, she looked like she was lying on top of a board. She amazed all of us. When it comes to life, why do some people seem like they are floating on top of the waves of life unbothered by the turmoil below, while others seem to sink into the water absorbed by the circumstances around them?

During an incident recorded for us, Jesus and His disciples were traveling by boat when a storm suddenly came up on the lake. Huge waves swept over them. Those hazardous storms were known to frequently cause shipwrecks and even loss of life. Jesus was sleeping through it all, frustrating His anxious and frightened disciples. Although He didn't sleep much longer. "The disciples woke him and said to him, "Teacher, don't you care if we drown?" He got up, rebuked the wind and said to the waves, "Quiet! Be still!" Then the wind died down and it was completely calm" Mark 4:38-39. Jesus had released peace over the storm. What an awesome display of His authority and power to rule over the laws of creation, as well as His desire to intervene for His disciples. It was prophesied of Jesus: "You rule over the surging sea; when its waves mount up, you still them" Psalm 89:9.

The disciples' destiny had been challenged—they were headed to the other side of the lake before the storm rose up to try to stop them. Our problems often seem like unending storms trying to stop or swallow us. Perhaps we have more control over our situations than we think we do, especially when we call on Jesus. God's goodness causes the storms of distraction, conflict and turmoil to be calmed in our lives. Let's learn a lesson from this incident and make Him our main focus.

Healthy Doubt

To doubt means to be uncertain about; to consider questionable or unlikely; to hesitate to believe. It also means to distrust. The positive side of doubt is that it can lead you to seek proof as to whether something is true or not. This keeps you from believing lies and half-truths. Doubt or being unsure can keep you from making mistakes. If you have a decision to make and you feel uncertain about what you should do, or feel doubtful that you are making the right decision, then the doubt or disquiet feeling acts as your alarm. It is a warning signal to reconsider the decision, or to stop and wait until there is assurance or a sense of peace about the decision or choice made.

Doubt can come in handy at other times too. Since the Bible warns of false teachers, it is a good thing when doubt leads to a search to verify whether a teaching is right or not. In Acts 17:11, we read about a sect of people who let doubt lead them to the Scriptures for verification: "Now the Berean Jews were of more noble character than those in Thessalonica, for they received the message with great eagerness and examined the Scriptures every day to see if what Paul said was true."

Unhealthy Doubt

Going back in history, we find in the very beginning, a crafty deceiver arriving on the scene and with subtle accusations put doubts in the minds of the first man and woman. He asked, "Did God really say...?" He made this couple wonder if God was being completely truthful and honest with them. This masked deceiver was accusing God of lying when in fact he was the real liar.

The truth of the matter is that this cunning one, who accused God before man, now stands before God and accuses us. He is the original liar and deceiver, not God. Have we fallen for his deception even today? How many still say in their hearts, "Did God really say...?" Do we doubt instead of believing the Word of God? Do we doubt God is who He says He is? Do we doubt He can to do the things He said He could do?

Sometimes people give only lip service. They express with their words, "I love you," but it never shows in their actions. Instead, feelings of rejection, being ignored or unloved ensues. They do not care or believe what you have to say. Your likes or dislikes, feelings and opinions mean nothing to them. In contrast, loving involves listening, understanding and responding in a positive way. Do your words tell God you love Him and do your actions follow suit?

God regularly went to the Garden of Eden to spend time with the first couple, Adam and Eve. When they first sinned, they hid in shame from Him. Do you hide from Him when He looks forward to being with you? He is all-powerful and has all authority, yet He extends grace and mercy. Do you recognize His love as well as His power? When people decide not to believe Him, it is the same as rejecting Him. If this is the case, they are also rejecting His love and power to make a difference in their lives.

God tells us that He is our heavenly Father and we are His children, if we have accepted His Son. Yet, how often does He observe people proceeding to ignore, reject and turn their backs on Him. Instead of understanding His will and His heart, and looking forward to His blessings and promises, they act as if He is a burden. They view Him as a God to accept, but they don't understand the closeness that can be established. Others deny He even exists.

The truth is He wants you to know Him personally, to understand His heart. He is looking and waiting for you to come to Him. Pastor Darrell Morgan of Word of Life Church in Apopka, Florida received this heavenly vision:

> God took me to His throne room where we had an extended conversation. Then Jesus asked, "Why don't the people listen to me?"
> "I don't know," I answered.

"Why don't the people listen to me?" He asked again.

"I don't know."

Then the emotional pain of the Lord overwhelmed me and I wept and wept.

You may think God is far away and isn't concerned about you, but that is not true. He loves you so much and looks forward to spending time with you. His desire is to be a loving and caring father to you, as well as your God. He wants you to have an abundant life, not one good day or one good year, but for life. He wants to give you peace. He wants you to have joy. It is time to take the limits off a limitless God. It is time to walk with Him hand-in-hand. It is time.

It is time to take the limits off a limitless God.

> "You make known to me the path of life;
> you will fill me with joy in your presence,
> with eternal pleasures at your right hand."
> Psalm 16:11

Without a Doubt

One major obstacle that gets in the way of faith is doubt. Even though we love God, do we turn around and doubt His Word, and question His ability to help us manage circumstances when things get rough?

Doubting God's ability often brings feelings of hopelessness and despair. A group of people from long ago had the same problem we often do in dealing with this five-letter word.

They grumbled and complained, doubting God's ability even after witnessing many miracles. They willfully tested Him and spoke against Him by the questions they asked, revealing that they did not understand His great desire and awesome ability to take care of them. They continually responded by asking, "Can God…?" What was their problem? They did not believe He could really take care of them. They did not trust in His deliverance. See Psalm 78:22. James tells us:

> "But when you ask, you must believe and not doubt, because the one who doubts is like a wave of the sea, blown and tossed by the wind. That person should not expect to receive anything from the Lord. Such a person is double-minded and unstable in all they do."
> James 1:6-8

When doubt in the Lord overtakes our thoughts, we can go to Him and ask forgiveness for our unbelief. Reading God's Word will plant it in our hearts and minds. It will begin to grow in our spirits as we speak it, hear it and do it. Believing and trusting are not passive; it is what we do. It is the action of expecting God to show up at any moment. When we expect Him, He will show up. He works in our lives, even if it is behind the scenes.

Did you realize it is possible for doubt and unbelief to keep away miracles? Jesus would have liked to perform more miracles in His hometown, but the people took offense instead of trusting Him. "And he did not do many miracles there because of their lack of faith" Matthew 13:58. Yet many times, He will bless us and intervene in our lives in spite of those bits of doubt, because of His great mercy and love.

At certain times in our lives, we all have difficulty with doubt. The key is in recognizing it and dealing with it immediately. Replace those first fleeting doubts that cross your mind with the Word of God. Take all your questions, doubts and fears to the Lord. He will blow them away and give you peace: peace in your heart, in your mind and in your soul.

He is the awesome, powerful creator of the entire universe. Is He able? Of course! He waits to hear from you and answer your prayers. He loves you! He would like you to have every good thing. The Holy Spirit's power will assist you with replacing doubt that disappoints, with faith in a caring, loving and very powerful God.

A Stretch of Faith

The cousin of Jesus, known as John the Baptist, had been telling King Herod, the ruler of Galilee, that it was not lawful for him to marry the woman who was now his wife. As expected, the king and his wife were not happy about this at all. As a favor to his wife, King Herod had John the Baptist imprisoned and eventually beheaded. John's disciples requested his body and after they buried him, they went to inform Jesus what had happened.

Hearing the news about the death of His cousin, Jesus looked forward to spending some time alone. He started out for a remote area by boat. In the meantime, the people from many of the surrounding towns heard where He was going and followed Him on foot. Seeing the huge crowd, Jesus had compassion on them and took time to heal their sick, putting aside His own desires for the moment.

On top of that, Jesus instructed His disciples to feed this crowd, which consisted of more than five thousand men in addition to women and children. His disciples objected. They only had five loaves of bread and two fish. Jesus was not concerned and had the people sit down on the grass. He took the small amount of bread and fish, and blessed them. He then broke the loaves in pieces and had the disciples distribute them to the people. The result of His faith was miraculous, "They all ate and were satisfied, and the disciples picked up twelve basketfuls of broken pieces that were left over" Matthew 14:20. What an awesome miracle!

Do things like this happen today? A friend volunteered for an organization that provided meals for the needy in our city. This particular day, more people than usual came looking for a warm meal. The huge pot of soup was almost empty. Yet the people kept streaming in. After a quick prayer, they continued to scoop out soup, and it never ran out until the last person was served!

Going back to Matthew 14, Jesus then dismissed the crowd. He sent His disciples back to their boat, telling them He would meet them on the other side of the lake later that night. Finally alone, He went up the mountainside to spend some time in prayer. As night fell, the boat with the disciples was already far from land. Rising strong winds pushed and pounded at their boat, as they fought the surging waves. Shortly before dawn, Jesus went out to them taking the straight path—straight across the lake. As He walked on the lake, He ignored the ripples beneath His feet as they lapped at His heels, as if to call Him down with them. He seemed unconcerned about the brewing storm. Imagine how terrified His disciples must have been when they saw Him walking on the water during this stormy night. They thought they were seeing a ghost.

"Take courage! It is I. Don't be afraid," Jesus immediately said to them.

"Lord, if it's you," Peter replied, "tell me to come to you on the water."

"Come."

Peter got down out of the boat, walked on the water and came toward Jesus. He literally walked on water. Imagine having that experience! However, his story continued. When he saw the wind and high waves, he became afraid.

"Lord, save me!" he shouted, as he began to sink.

"You of little faith," Jesus said, "why did you doubt?"

Immediately Jesus reached out His hand and caught him. Jesus and Peter climbed into the boat and the wind died down. The others in the boat were awestruck, excitedly crying out, "You really are the Son of God!"

With total confidence in his friend and Lord, Peter had walked out to meet Him. As long as his eyes remained on Jesus, he was fine. But it was not long before he started looking at his surroundings. He felt the wind. He saw the waves. He probably thought, "I'm not supposed to be able to do this." Doubt quickly took over as he became frightened. Taking his attention off Jesus, he began to sink into the churning dark water, but Jesus came to his rescue.

Henry Ford unknowingly summed up Peter's experience when he said, "Whether you think that you can or that you can't, you are usually right." Be inspired by this event in Peter's life to keep your eyes off the circumstances and focused on Jesus.

Leap of Faith

In Hebrews 11:1, we read, "Now faith is confidence in what we hope for and assurance about what we do not see." The faith we need is not in ourselves and it is not in others. It is not in people's wisdom. It is in God. Paul put it this way, "so that your faith might not rest on human wisdom, but on God's power" 1 Corinthians 2:5. If you love Him, trust Him and believe His Word. Confidence in His mighty, awesome power brings His intervention in to your life and even more than that, it pleases Him: "And without faith it is impossible to please God, because anyone who comes to him must believe that he exists and that he rewards those who earnestly seek him" Hebrews 11:6.

We show faith by believing what He says. We look to Him instead of focusing on the situation, even if we are still waiting for His answer or the way out isn't clear yet. Have full assurance in His ability to reveal that way. Once we receive the answer or solution then faith isn't needed any longer. David tells us what to expect when we seek and depend on the Lord, "I sought the Lord, and he answered me; he delivered me from all my fears" Psalm 34:4. He also wrote, "You have delivered me from all my troubles" Psalm 54:7.

Along with many others, I lost my job in the 2008 economy slow-down. Unemployment checks brought relief for a while, but they would soon run out. Positive results to the resumes I continually sent out were not coming in. I was becoming concerned and concern soon turned into worry. Admittedly, I began to fear the ramifications of no income for the bills that would be coming due. As I talked with the Lord, I kept in mind that I could count on Him to provide for my needs. And He did just that; I received a job in time to keep all my commitments.

In Mark 11:12-14, we read about the incident of Jesus and the fig tree. As Jesus and His disciples were walking along, they saw a fig tree in the distance. The fig tree's leaves announced the arrival of figs. Approaching it, Jesus found it did not have any figs at all. He cursed the tree for its deception. The following morning, the disciples discovered the tree had withered from its roots. Remembering what Jesus had said to the tree, Peter pointed it out to Him. The response from Jesus gives quite an example of the power of faith:

> "Have faith in God," Jesus answered. "Truly I tell you, if anyone says to this mountain, 'Go, throw yourself into the sea,' and does not doubt in his heart but believes that what they say will happen, it will be done for them. Therefore I tell you, whatever you ask for in prayer, believe that you have received it, and it will be yours." Mark 11:22-24

Mountains can represent problems that come into our lives. Do your problems seem like mountains to you at times? Do they seem like there is no way to get over them, through them or around them, or that they are just overwhelming in magnitude? Tell your problem—your mountain—that it no longer has control over your life, because you gave the Lord full control to work in that situation. We all have a choice to make—to live by fear or to live by faith. Step out and take the leap of faith, faith in the One who loves you.

Wounded Hearts

A wise man once said:

"There is a time for everything,
and a season for every activity under the heavens:
a time to be born and a time to die,
a time to plant and a time to uproot,
a time to kill and a time to heal,
a time to tear down and a time to build,
a time to weep and a time to laugh,
a time to mourn and a time to dance,
a time to scatter stones and a time to gather them,
a time to embrace and a time to refrain from embracing,
a time to search and a time to give up,
a time to keep and a time to throw away,
a time to tear and a time to mend,
a time to be silent and a time to speak,
a time to love and a time to hate,
a time for war and a time for peace."
Ecclesiastes 3:1-8

My interpretation of this quote is *stuff happens*. Some things just happen; we have no control over them. And other things we can control or influence. Different things that happen in life teach us about human nature. We learn what people can be like with or without God in their lives, and what they can be like with or without following His way of love towards one another.

We could ask ourselves if a bad experience has something to learn from it. Think about ways to avoid a similar situation, if possible, then plan to implement that way in the future. Whatever your own life hurt has been, whether an abusive situation, hurtful words, rejection, an injustice or losing someone close, time is needed to process it and heal.

Look forward to the time when the pain isn't controlling your every thought or keeping you from moving into a better future. If a past hurtful memory rises up to flood your mind, it is all right to accept it for a moment. Acknowledge the pain and the hurt that came from that experience. Then deal with the harassing memory by reminding it, it is no longer a part of your present.

Wounds to your heart could have been unintentional, but it wounded nevertheless. An accident may have taken the life of a loved one, but it was still an accident. Then again, there may be times when the hurt was intentional. In either case, your heart requires time to heal. Time to grieve may also be necessary, especially when the loss of a loved one is involved or a relationship ends. Talk to God about these situations and personally forgive those involved, including yourself if need be.

A Time to Forgive

Forgiving is for your healing. It is not condoning the wrong. It is not saying it was right or OK. Any hurtful deed is not acceptable. Forgive by giving the situation to the Lord to handle. The act of forgiving releases those involved from continuing to control your mind, your feelings and your future. They are no longer accountable to you; instead, they are accountable to God for their actions.

We are told revenge belongs to Him alone: "Do not take revenge, my dear friends, but leave room for God's wrath, for it is written: "It is mine to avenge; I will repay," says the Lord"

Romans 12:19. In 1 Thessalonians 5:15, we read, "Make sure that nobody pays back wrong for wrong, but always strive to do what is good for each other and for everyone else."

These Scriptures relieve us from the bitterness, resentment and anger that may lead to unlawful reactions or consequences on our part. It does not mean that a person should not or does not pay consequences for wrongs done or laws broken. Our law systems bring justice, as well as God stepping in. In Hebrews 10:31, we read, "It is a dreadful thing to fall into the hands of the living God." Colossians 3:25 says, "Anyone who does wrong will be repaid for their wrongs, and there is no favoritism." It is quite evident that we do not have to think, "They are getting away with it."

You might ask, "What if the offending person isn't even sorry or hasn't sought my forgiveness?" It doesn't really matter, because that person has to stand before God. Think of forgiving as a gift to yourself. Choosing forgiveness releases you from the control that situation or person had over your thoughts and feelings. It will benefit your own soul. Otherwise, you will feel stuck in time.

And please, never blame God for unfortunate situations that come from mistakes of others or even from your own mistakes, unwise choices or wrong desires. What happens is not always His will, just because He refrains from intervening or allows life to take its course. Physical and spiritual principles and laws have been set in place since creation. Whether they are followed, broken or misused determine many of the good or bad things that happen around us. One evening I heard the Lord say:

> "My approval is not stamped on all the events that have taken place, that are forming or

that will take place. They are man's will, consequences of his decisions. There are times my intervention is sought and there are times I choose to intervene. This is my prerogative, for you are my creation."

Our Reactions

Reactions to tragedy come in many forms. One mother had lost her beloved son to a terrible driving accident. She became angry with God. How dare He take her son from her. Why didn't He protect him or save him? All very natural questions. The pain and heartache from some losses never completely disappears. But when the grieving process is cut short, complete healing is not achieved; acceptance and closure are never reached. This grieving mother would not allow herself to be comforted. She stopped attending church with her husband and lived her life in despair, confining herself to her home.

In contrast, another woman lost her precious daughter at the hands of an abusive man. In time, this grieving, distressed mother was able to visit the prison where this horrible man was serving his sentence. She chose to visit him there on several occasions. She came to the place she could finally forgive him. Eventually she offered him the knowledge of God's plan, leading to his salvation.

A father lost his son at the hands of an angry mob. As the son lay dying he cried out for his father, but in that moment, his father could not save him. Time passed. This incredibly merciful man was able to meet with each person who was responsible for the death of his beloved and only son. One by one, as their hearts convicted them of their guilt for what they had done, this father gave them his forgiveness. In addition, he befriended them. On top of that, he treated them as if they were his own sons. Incredible, isn't it? It is almost unthinkable that someone could do this. In reality, this is exactly what God did for us. It is what He did for you. The father in this story represents our heavenly Father, and the man's son represents Jesus.

The presence of God draws us forward, while our pain draws us backward. We were created to live in His presence where healing is found. You are here for a reason. He has a good purpose for your life. What are you doing with yours? Are you wasting it on regrets and worries? Are you stuck because of fear? Try relying on God and His promises. He has called you to a higher purpose, one that is ahead of you, not behind you.

Chapter 4

A Balancing Act

It was fun balancing on the curb of the long sidewalk outside my grandparents' home. My brother and I followed each other in a little row as my younger sister tried to keep up. On excursions to the playground, we balanced on the narrow wall that went along the grassy banks of well-groomed yards.

On an outing to the circus, the tightrope performers held my attention. From my seat below, it appeared they balanced on a thin string. From a documentary about the training of circus people to become the professional performers they are, I watched tightrope walkers start their training with a rope barely a foot off the ground. As they gained confidence and balance, the rope moved higher and higher. A safety net hung below the rope as it rose higher above the ground. These specially trained men and women held a balancing rod to stabilize their movements, as they crossed the thin rope to entertain their fans.

I often feel like life is a balancing act with all its difficulties. Balancing on the curb, wall or tightrope represents for me the narrow road. Every time I lose my balance and slip off, the broad road waits. Occasionally I feel like I spend more time falling onto the broad road, but I prefer staying on the tightrope, following the narrow road. Jesus said:

> "Enter through the narrow gate. For wide is the gate and broad is the road that leads to destruction, and many enter through it. But small is the gate and narrow the road that leads to life and only a few find it." Matthew 7:13-14

I once contemplated my life with all its up and downs: the sad times and happy times, the frustrating times and peaceful times. Then it occurred to me how the choices we make can easily lead to a life of destruction filled with everything we do not want. On the other hand, our choices can also lead to a better life, the one we do want. The choices and decisions others make may also affect our lives along the way. Decisions made without foresight, understanding or knowledge lead through the wide gate onto the broad road. In contrast, the life led with focus, wisdom and love lead through the small gate along the narrow road.

The struggle to get back up on that thin rope, the narrow path, only to lose your balance and fall off once again, can become overwhelming, frustrating and sometimes seem impossible. But you have a safety net to catch you when you fall—His name is Jesus. And He has the strength and ability to lift you back up on the tightrope, back on the narrow path when you feel too weak to get up yourself. The Holy Spirit has the power to keep you on the narrow path with His direction and guidance, becoming your balancing rod, your stabilizer. And so my prayer has become, "Thank you Lord for your strength and thank you Holy Spirit for your direction."

When Jesus becomes your Savior and the Holy Spirit comes to live in you, be aware that God will be with you in every situation, whether good or bad. Possibly, you are not on an easy road at this time, but He is there with you. Hold on to that. In addition, it is not necessary to do everything on your own. Your heavenly Father sent the Holy Spirit to assist you along the way. Look to Him for direction.

Unfortunately, life is not always wonderful, no matter how much we would like it to be. Life is not always easy and that is OK, because our experiences become our story. The hard times build our character and purify us, if we let them. Those times become an opportunity to become better and wiser.

Do you feel you need more wisdom? James wrote, "If any of you lacks wisdom, you should ask God, who gives generously to all without finding fault, and it will be given to you" James 1:5. Gaining wisdom will also help us to keep from slipping off the right path. Sololmon wrote, "I instruct you in the way of wisdom and lead you along straight paths. When you walk, your steps will not be hampered; when you run, you will not stumble" Proverbs 4:11-12.

Too often, we make left turns and right turns, instead of forging straight ahead. Taking side trips only makes the way harder and complicated. As we put our hands in God's, He will guide and lead us. With Him, it is not hard. It is not complicated. He lays our path out straight ahead of us, but we have to walk in it. His way is before us; let's walk straight ahead with Him.

A Fall off the Wall

The traffic was moving extra slowly. Turning on the car radio, I heard Chuck Swindoll, founder of *Insight for Living*, talking about the childhood rhyme of Humpty Dumpty.

> Humpty Dumpty sat on a wall,
> Humpty Dumpty had a great fall.
> All the King's horses, And all the King's men
> Couldn't put Humpty together again.

He finished his version of the rhyme by saying, "Christ came to our wall to pick up our fall." His statement reminded me of the following Scripture: "The Lord is trustworthy in all he promises and faithful in all he does. The Lord upholds all who fall and lifts up all who are bowed down" Psalm 145:13-14. He wants to lift you up from the problems, sadness, despair or whatever it is that is weighing you down.

You are not alone. David wrote, "But you, Lord, are a shield around me, my glory, the One who lifts my head high. I call out to the Lord, and he answers me from his holy mountain" Psalm 3:3-4. Put your hand in His and let Him guide you and lead you.

A Bout with Cancer

The tests were over. The results were in. Waiting in the sterile room, I hoped for the best. Instead, I heard those fateful words, "You have cancer." It was late in 2003 when I was diagnosed with colon cancer. It had already migrated through the intestinal wall and entered the majority of lymph nodes tested. Stage three. I listened to the percentage of the chances I had of living or dying, given dutifully and sensitively by my gastrologist. Visiting my oncologist later that day, he proceeded to tell me the probability of it coming back even if I made it through the chemo. I had decided not to accept less than a positive outcome for my life, so hearing those statistics made me angry.

Even though I knew the doctors were being upfront with me, their words were now ringing in my ears, tearing down my confidence and my hope. This bombardment of negative statistics occupied my mind. I needed the power of those words broken off my life. Are you aware of the power that is in the words we speak? It is possible to build up or discourage others by what we say. I soon went to visit our assistant pastor for prayer. Finally, those statements stopped their endless swirling in my mind.

I knew the name of Jesus was greater than the name of any disease. I knew my God created my body and could heal whatever came against it. I knew He was with me during the month I spent in the hospital going through two major operations, and during the months of life-draining chemotherapy that followed. God gives doctors and nurses special talents and abilities for their noble professions. My excellent doctors were a tool in His hands to bring restoration to my body. The dedicated nurses were an enormous encouragement to me.

What a surprise when young students stopped by my hospital room to add a bit of cheer. One student came in with her paint set and canvas paper, and made a picture from colors of my choosing. Another student brought in his instrument to serenade me with a beautiful song. Such selfless acts meant so much. The hospital Chaplain, a young man on his way to finding his destiny, stopped to visit and pray for me. I'm sure God gave special blessings to each one. In addition, the love and support of family and friends meant the world to me. How could I ask for more?

During that time, my hope was entrenched in knowing God needed me here a little while longer. When I felt too weak to go on, I looked to Him for strength to see me through. I pictured myself reaching my hand up to hold His, and when I felt too weak to even envision lifting my hand I knew He was reaching down to hold mine. He was my rock and my strength.

> "For I am the Lord your God
> who takes hold of your right hand
> and says to you, Do not fear;
> I will help you." Isaiah 41:13

Many times, I would envision friends from around the world praying for me when I felt too weak to pray. I'd see myself resting behind their shields of faith. This was a vision my pastor told me to hang on to, and I took advantage of that vision on many occasions; how comforting it was.

If anyone you know hears the words, "You have cancer," realize it doesn't necessarily mean a death sentence, or from any other disease for that matter. Let your words support and promote life and your prayers flow on their behalf to the throne of God. That is when miracles happen, and we all wish for a miracle now and then. Think about this—in order to receive a miracle there has to be a problem.

Concerning sickness, God's ultimate will is for us to be well. The willingness of Jesus to give His life for us brought us spiritual healing and eternal life. His willingness to suffer beatings and physical abuse before His crucifixion paid the price for our physical healing. It was prophesied of Jesus:

> "But he was pierced for our transgressions,
> he was crushed for our iniquities;
> the punishment that brought us peace was on him,
> and by his wounds we are healed." Isaiah 53:5

Long ago, God identified Himself by saying, "I am the Lord, who heals you" Exodus 15:26. The Psalmist wrote, "Praise the LORD, my soul, and forget not all his benefits—who forgives all your sins and heals all your diseases" Psalm 103:2-3. Jesus demonstrated God's heart when He walked on this earth performing miracles of healing: "Jesus went through all the towns and villages, teaching in their synagogues, proclaiming the good news of the kingdom and healing every disease and sickness" Matthew 9:35.

From the beginning, God created in us an immune system to help eliminate harmful things from our bodies. When that system becomes overloaded with toxins and stress, adverse symptoms result. There are times God intercedes in a person's life and performs a miracle healing and the physical problem disappears without intervention. Sometimes strengthening the immune system helps the body rid itself of sickness producing organisms. Other times, He gives doctors the wisdom and skill needed to aid those who are sick or injured. Others receive their healing as they stand face to face with the Lord. Whether it is here or in heaven, our healing will come. When we have given the Lord our hearts, the greatest event occurs the moment we step from this life into the next. We win either way.

My bout with cancer was not a fun experience, but it most definitely was a wake-up call. My heart was drawn more to the people in my life rather than to the busyness that had filled it. It led me to do extensive research on nutrition and the effect different foods and stress have on our bodies. Most important, I trusted God as my healer and in His purpose for my life. I praise and thank the Lord for His loving kindness. But whether I stayed here or had gone to be with Him, I knew He would always have His arms of love wrapped tightly around me and for that, I will be eternally grateful.

Fly and Soar

It was a breezy, sunny day as I sat on an old wooden bench beside the lake in Mt. Dora. The struggling birds flying above the rippling water fascinated me. The birds flying against the wind were flapping their wings like crazy. Yet they hardly inched forward. Despite all their striving, they were not getting any closer to their destination. As tiredness overtook them and the flapping of wings slowed, the wind blew them backward. One faltering bird, blown downward, struggled to gain control of his wings, and then began again the constant flapping.

Another type of bird was flying in the direction the wind was blowing. These birds barely needed to flap their wings. Most of the time they just spread them out and glided as the wind carried them along. There was no plummeting downward or backward, no struggle, striving and fighting against the wind.

How often are you like the struggling birds flying against the wind? Do you feel like you are constantly struggling and working hard, yet never seem to get anywhere? Do you begin to break down as your life takes one nosedive after another?

Does life seem overwhelming? Not knowing how to handle the problems that come our way, we plummet under the pressure, working even harder to keep our heads above water.

The birds flying with the wind were not struggling. They were just going with the flow. In fact, they were speeding forward at an accelerated rate without even trying. They were at peace, at rest, as they glided and soared above the problems going on beside them and below them. When we follow the higher thoughts and ways of God, we are like the birds going with the flow above the turmoil. Following many of the thoughts and ways of men lead us into all sorts of problems, like the birds flying and struggling against the wind.

Throughout the Bible, God reveals His thoughts and teaches us His ways. A renewing of our minds begins to take place after we accept Jesus as our Savior and Lord. As we read His Word, verbalize it, listen to it and do it, it becomes firmly planted in our minds and hearts. Doing these things makes understanding His thoughts and applying His ways to our lives much easier.

You have a loving and caring heavenly Father who loves you, wants to take care of you and be involved in your life. If you had a father who rejected or abused you, you may say to yourself, "If God is anything like my father then I don't want to have anything to do with Him." Understand this—He is everything you wanted your real dad to be and more.

Why try to handle and work out problems that come your way by yourself? I know how grateful I have been to have Him to turn to and lean on. My best advice: Follow Him, run to Him. He has all you could want and all you will ever need. He invites you to come and bask in the love He has for you. See Him for who He is—your heavenly Father who cares for you. Let Him hold you, lift you up and wipe your tears away. Allow Him to strengthen you and teach you. He is calling to you and wooing you to come to Him and experience His great love.

Fly and soar with the Lord, riding the clouds above the turmoil where it is smooth and peaceful. Everything you desire and need is obtained through Him. God's love takes you higher. The Lord is calling you to come by His side, to come up higher with Him into a higher place of understanding and thinking. I heard the Lord say:

> "I am in the storms of life: watching, building, sorting, deciding, planning. Come up higher in your thinking. Come up with me where the sky meets the heavens. Your world is small. Expand your horizons and see as I see. See the expanse of the universe. I've created it all. The small things are but a drop in the bucket, a drop in time. Stretch your world and live in mine. Rise above the storms. Never turn back, move only forward. Come here where I wait for you in my sanctuary of love. Come up higher and sail with me above all that displease you, above the hurts and the pains."

It is time to climb the stairs to His kingdom. Frustration is not part of your destiny. As you live in the present, also rise above the things that frustrate and make you anxious. Rise above the circumstances and move in the Spirit realm by turning your attention to God's kingdom, a kingdom that is full of life, love and abundance for here and now. Sweep away the crumbs of the past. Hold His hand and walk into your future. Discover peace and rest soaring above the problems of life as you go with the flow, walking hand-in-hand with your God.

PART 2

Over The Bumps

You laid your eternity in His hands,
So put today in His hands, too.

Chapter 5

Twists and Turns

I prefer to live in a world filled with kind, caring and loving people, and have a great and lovely life. Only there is no fighting reality. Instead of wanting to live in a fantasy world, I found it is better to face reality. Life includes bad times and good times. It is not a straight road. Curves wind around obstacles, tunnels plow through obstacles, bumps and hills rise up. Negative events, wrong beliefs, assumptions, comparisons and prejudices hinder us from moving forward to accomplish what we really long for in life, or from experiencing the full life that is waiting for us.

Babies wobble and fall down as they grow and begin to stand and walk. Not to be defeated, these little ones get up and start all over again. With bright eyes and gleeful smiles, they triumph as they stand all by themselves. It is exciting to watch those first few attempts. Wobble, wobble, then down they go. With each try, they became stronger and able to stand longer, occasionally attempting to take a few steps forward.

Growing into the toddler stage, they soon walk with only an occasional fall. As they reach childhood, they are not only standing and walking; they are running, skipping, hopping and jumping. In adulthood, the times are rare when they trip or fall. If it does happen, they pick themselves up, brush themselves off, heal if they have to, and then just keep on going.

This procedure is like the counterpart to our spiritual walk. As we begin to walk in the steps of Jesus, we may wobble and fall at times, but His forgiveness picks us up and dusts us off. We become stronger as we hold our heavenly Father's hand for support. We are cheered on as we keep trying and moving forward. It becomes continually easier as we move away from the falls and closer to spiritual maturity.

Some people go their own way and tumble through life, tossed back and forth this way and that way. They often wonder why life has to be so difficult and tire of hoping for a future or a dream that never seems to come. They get tired of arguing with their spouse and correcting the kids. Feelings of frustration and anger become their friends. One problem tumbles upon another. How many have asked, "Is this all there is?"

Has life become so overwhelming that you have entertained the thought, "I might as well give up and quit trying?" What if a toddler would sit down and give up, thinking it was impossible for him to walk without falling? With this response, the toddler would cripple himself for the rest of his life. He never would accomplish and enjoy all he could have.

Even though you may face disappointment, criticism, frustration or pain, never permit it to stop you. The Bible's wisdom encourages you not to stay down, but to continue to get up as many times as it takes: "For though the righteous fall seven times, they rise again" Proverbs 24:16. So if you get knocked down, get up again and keep on going.

Life is like being on a road that twists and turns through the countryside. As my son was going through some difficult times, it occurred to me that life is also a bit like the jumping beans I played with as a child. It may wobble and turn upside down, but eventually it turns right side up again. Just remember: it is important not to leave God out, no matter which way your life wobbles.

The Dust Storm

> "When Jesus spoke again to the people, he said, "I am the light of the world. Whoever follows me will never walk in darkness, but will have the light of life." John 8:12

I was wounded and hurting. I opened my mouth and out spilled anger, resentment and accusations. They came rolling out like a dust storm, blowing out the dirt from the very bottom of my heart. Instead of being whisked away with the breeze, the dirt settled back down and covered me with its suffocating dusty coat.

Could the sweeper draw this dirt away from me? No. Could water wash it all away? No. What would, then? Only forgiveness could take it away with its spiritually fortified, dissolving power. I poured in forgiveness, letting it settle and sit in the bottom recesses of my dying soul. Its scouring power slowly dissolved the anger, the resentment and the accusations. Compassion, love and mercy began to fill me and flow freely from my mouth. They were like bursts of light radiating from the bottom of my heart, recovered and joyful. The light encircled me like the warm sunshine on a sunny, spring day. The light wiped out the dust storm and it ceased to exist. Forgiveness triumphed once again!

In Colossians 3:13, we read, "Bear with each other and forgive one another if any of you has a grievance against someone. Forgive as the Lord forgave you." Jesus went further saying, "But I tell you, love your enemies and pray for those who persecute you, that you may be children of your Father in heaven" Matthew 5:44-45. One way we can show love towards our enemies is by praying for them. This Scripture also reveals God's tremendous patience and love for all of us. Pastor Vernon Rainwater of Northland Church in Longwood, Florida said, "We may not think others deserve Jesus, but He thinks they do."

Sometimes it takes years to come to a place where you can extend forgiveness to someone who has wounded you. It is a process and it takes time to work through painful memories in order to heal. Although the memory and effects of abuse can last for years, it is possible to move through the process of forgiving. As a side note, forgiving does not condone what was done, and it does not mean you put yourself back into a dangerous or abusive situation.

Jesus never asks us to do anything He didn't do first. One day the people were praising Him as a king and the next day they were calling for His death. Falsely accused during an illegal trial, the judge pronounced Him guilty. The death sentence followed. As His last breath left His body, He uttered these words: "Father, forgive them, for they do not know what they are doing" Luke 23:34. And even more awesome than this, Jesus willingly paid our death sentence for us, the punishment we deserved for our sins. This enabled God to offer us forgiveness for the sins and wrongs we committed.

We can't change the past, but we can create a new one. Although we don't have the power to limit ourselves to only great memories, we have the opportunity to create joyful and pleasant memories every day. It is time to get in the race and stop looking at what is behind. "Let us run with perseverance the race marked out for us, fixing our eyes on Jesus, the pioneer and perfecter of faith. For the joy set before him he endured the cross, scorning its shame, and sat down at the right hand of the throne of God" Hebrews 12:1-2.

Sore Spots

I frequently told my children to pick up their shoes and put them away, hoping someday it would eventually become a habit. One morning, I tripped over a pair of my own shoes and broke a toe on my right foot, as well as damaging some of the nerves and blood vessels on the top of my foot. My children will never let me live it down. Even now that they are grown, from time to time they bring it up. For some reason they found the incident very funny. My throbbing, hurting toe did not find it so amusing. The smallest bump, even the slightest touch to my hurt toe would cause pain to go racing through my body bringing yelps of pain. It was not a happy toe. Once it healed, a bump or touch practically went unnoticed.

Our hearts react in a similar manner. When we see in others the smallest tendency towards a way of acting or a characteristic that led to previous hurt in our lives, it causes us to think that this person might do the same. Our sensitive hearts begin to holler, "Be careful. Watch out." This may be a good thing. It becomes a thermometer to protect us. On the other hand, the unchecked and unhealed hurting heart can lead to condemning prejudices and unrestrained complaints toward people who may not even deserve it.

Although it is important to take our cares to the Lord, He does not want bombarded with constant complaining and whining. I remember a time when I heard the phrase, "Stop your bellyaching," three times within a day and a half. I thought to myself, "I think God must be trying to tell me something." I am sure He was telling me that my complaining had to go. At times, it is better to keep our peace and not say anything. Complaining complicates matters, while an attitude of gratitude and thankfulness lessens the burdens and soothes the soul. It also does not deliver us from the enemy. To see victory, it is more beneficial to get God's strategy and look to the Holy Spirit to lead us. God enjoys our company, so ask Him for His strategy when fighting battles.

David wrote, "The LORD is close to the brokenhearted and saves those who are crushed in spirit. The righteous person may have many troubles, but the LORD delivers him from them all" Psalm 34:18-19. To be brokenhearted means the heart, the mind and emotions are broken into pieces, crushed. Crushed in spirit means hope is gone. This Scripture even says a righteous man will have trouble, but the Lord adds that He will be there, offering solutions and assistance.

When we seek Him, our response changes and hope ensues. What has caused your sensitive areas, your sore spots? How do you respond? In Psalm 147:3, we read, "He heals the brokenhearted and binds up their wounds." Can you hear the Lord say:

> "I love you so much. Because you suffer, does not mean I don't love you. When a parent

watches his child trip and fall, it doesn't mean it was the parent's fault or that he doesn't love the child, because he didn't save him from tripping and falling. But you say to me, I guess God doesn't love me, because He let me trip and fall and I got hurt.

A loving parent will encourage the fallen child to get up and will tell him, he'll be ok. If it's needed, he will dress and bandage the wound, and it heals. And so, just as a loving parent, I encourage you to learn from those events that take place in your life. Come to me and let me hold you and bandage your wound. For have I not said, I bind up the wounds of the brokenhearted?"

It is time to yield the hurts and pains that linger in your heart, the offenses that still fester and the insults that still smart, to the One who is willing to carry your burdens for you. He cares about you. He can handle them all. His heart is not too small or His arms too short that He can't carry them for you.

Clinging to heartaches

Some people find releasing deep-seated hurts almost impossible, yet God did not intend for us to hold grudges. Often we keep our inner pain bottled up inside for so long, we can't find words to express how we feel. I want to encourage those who may be in a similar place that a time will come when those painful emotions will find release. Here is an excerpt from my own personal journal:

Oh, the anger and the pain, the hate, the bitterness that overwhelms my whole being. Feel the pain and sadness he brought into my life. Frustration envelopes me. Anger grows like its own being inside of me until I feel I will burst. How I want to run away and hide—to be alone to lick my wounds. My soul cries out to God. Save me from such undeserved treatment. Does God hear me? Where is He? I cannot shake this anger. It lingers on and on, year after year, eating away at my heart.

"Forgive."

Who says, "Forgive?" How can you know what I've suffered? I laugh in their faces. He deserves my anger. He deserves my hate. God should curse him. I ask God to let His revenge fall upon him.

Now he is gone. But wait, where is the peace? The anger, the pain, the bitterness all rage on. *Forgive* sounds so foreign to me. Is that a word I'm supposed to know? The flesh heals quickly, but my heart continues to bleed and my soul continues to weep. Will healing ever come? The anger eats away at me. Help me Lord! Where is your peace?

"Forgive."

I don't want to forgive. He doesn't deserve forgiveness. Look and see what he's done. See the pain he has caused my heart. Forgive? He's not even sorry. He feels no regret. He doesn't seek my forgiveness. Hate overpowers me. Lord, it hurts to hate so much. Time goes on. It doesn't heal the memories. I bury the anger. I hide the pain. But like a snake ready to attack, it rises to lash out; its venom poisoning my soul.

Lord, I need your forgiveness. Forgive me for hanging on to this anger that embitters me. It keeps me far from you. I miss feeling your closeness. Prayer is not easy in the midst of such hatred and anger. Yet, I find an odd sense of satisfaction by holding on to these feelings. After all, he deserves it and more.

"Forgive me Lord. Teach me to forgive."

Was I there to ask Christ's forgiveness as He was crucified for my sins? As His body was tortured and His breath left Him, was I there to say how sorry I was for all I did wrong? Was I so righteous and good that I didn't need to be pardoned. Scripture says, "all have sinned and fall short of the glory of God" Romans 3:23. I deserve death for my sins. Only Christ lived a sinless life, He deserved life. How great is His mercy and grace. How bountiful is His love to have taken my place on that dreadful cross. When I accept God's complete forgiveness for myself, how can I not forgive others?

Forgiveness: undeserved pardon. The vision of the cross led me to understand the concept of forgiveness. I am crucified with Christ and raised up to live a new life with faith in Him, making it possible for forgiveness to flow from my heart. I was hurt. He didn't deserve my pardon. But that's why it is called "forgiveness."

Clinging to heartaches is not beneficial. They will turn into your own private monsters. Emotional scars left me with years of resentment and bitterness. Yet the time came when I sensed God's arms open wide, and my hurting heart jumped into His arms to be consoled and comforted. It was on that day, He healed my broken heart. My anger and bitterness vanished as forgiveness and compassion toward others broke forth. The future took life in me as resentments and disappointments faded. Sadness dissolved as joy welled up in my heart. Peace overtook me. And, it all began the day I walked into God's love!

An Enemy

At one time, we probably all knew a bully bent on harassing and tormenting those around him. In the spiritual realm, there also exists a bully. He is called by various names. Some call him Satan and some call him the devil. Just as bullies often have their little pack of supporters, the devil has his as well, in the spiritual realm. They are known as demons or devils. They are actually fallen angels; angels who turned against the very God who made them, in order to follow one of their own, namely Satan.

The Bible tells us we have an enemy that roams around like a lion seeking whom he can devour. That enemy is Satan and his cohorts. They have no desire to see us serve the Lord or fulfill our destiny. They are jealous over the fact that God created us in His image. Therefore, they war against us, constantly finding the back roads and inroads into our lives to discourage us and pull us down. We must always be vigilant: "For our struggle is not against flesh and blood, but against the rulers, against the authorities, against the powers of this dark world and against the spiritual forces of evil in the heavenly realms" Ephesians 6:12.

John said of the devil: "He was a murderer from the beginning, not holding to the truth, for there is no truth in him. When he lies, he speaks his native language, for he is a liar and the father of lies" John 8:44. Jesus contrasted His purpose with the enemy's: "The thief's purpose is to steal, kill and destroy. My purpose is to give life in all its fullness" John 10:10 (TLB).

Satan is our enemy. His mission is to deceive, destroy and steal from us everything God intends for us to have. He not only wants to kill our bodies, but he wants to destroy our character and our opportunity to become all God desires us to be. Most of all, He wants to destroy our relationship with God, and he started this conquest from the very beginning with Adam and Eve, when he planted in their hearts doubt and distrust towards their maker.

If we decide to express words of doubt, fear and unbelief, it is like giving the devil the go ahead to attack us, because these expressions are not in agreement with God's Word. When everything is looking rosy, we speak life and joy out of our mouths. If the circumstance changes and things are not looking so rosy anymore, do we arm the enemy with weapons through our words? If we declare the Word of God one minute and the enemy's fearful lies the next, we give him ground into our lives. Don't allow the enemy to use your own words against you. Instead, speak words of faith and hope. Speak words that encourage and bring life.

The Snake

The cabin was a place for relaxation, a mini getaway from everyday life. Friends shared the cabin, enjoying the change of pace. The sun was glistening in the windows as it began to rise to its noonday stance. Suddenly, eyes grew big in disbelief. We stood paralyzed. A floorboard creaked as it moved and rose.

Emerging from this dark space was the huge head of a snake. Slithering from its hiding space, an enormous seemingly endless body pushed the snake's head along. We watched in horror as its body glided into the light, with the breaking and heaving of floorboards. It was determined its body was at least fourteen inches wide. With darting eyes, it made its way across the room, down the hall and filled the next room before its tail finally revealed itself above the floorboards.

We looked upon it in shock as well as in awe. It was quite a magnificent creature, a remarkable sight. Its scaly skin radiated with beautiful, vibrant, swirling colors. After catching my breath, I followed this beautiful, mysterious creature. Only to discover that in the next room it was wrapping itself around a man who came to enjoy a time of peace. Screams came from somewhere deep inside me as I witnessed this huge creature inserting its fangs again and again.

Looking around I saw the stuffed animals of a child scattered around the room. Plunging them, one after another, into the menacing mouth of this monster, I hoped to defray the torture this man was enduring. The creature was no longer beautiful in my sight. I saw only an ugly monster. A 911 call; a cry for help went out. This friend, now pale, seemed thinner as life drained from him. Black and blue marks covered his arms where fangs mercilessly attacked him.

"I'm fine," he said. "Don't worry about me." Incredibly he asked, "May I have a drink of water?" An unending avalanche of thoughts raced through my mind. I was confused, how could this be happening? There was no warning. It was an unforeseen vicious attack. How do I make this horrific scene go away? Can I pretend it never happened? The light from the window poured in upon my bed, forcing my eyes open. A dream! It was only a dream. But, was it—just a dream?

Our enemy lies in wait, waiting to break up our foundation with sin. With darting eyes he looks for those he can deceive. Without being recognized, He wounds with deceptions that run deep. His attack is vicious and without warning, a warning for us to be on guard every minute.

Friends betray friends. Members of families strike out at each other. Unfamiliar faces attack each other without warning. Lies, cheating, murder, stealing and a host of other sins fill this world, because of the evil gripping many hearts. Sin deceives, often seeming good, right or beautiful for a time. Nevertheless, in the end it destroys and becomes something very ugly.

Unaware of the influence of a deceptive spirit, the affected say, "Don't worry about me." "I'm fine." The addict, the offender, the abuser and the one that runs after evil continue on, going through the motions of everyday living. No one wants to envision, think about or consider the *thing* wrapping around them, sinking in its deadly fangs and stealing their very life away. Oblivious to this hidden monster they fall under its control. In the midst of sin, people may delude themselves in to thinking there isn't anything wrong. "And no wonder, for Satan himself masquerades as an angel of light" 2 Corinthians 11:14.

Innocent as children, many people overlook the reality of this terrible danger lurking nearby, preferring to pretend it doesn't exist. As the man in the dream relaxed, the enemy wrapped him in sin as his poison penetrated him. Innocence isn't effective against the devil. God's Word and His armor are needed. A 911 call goes out to God. It is shocking to see sin come into the light of day. When the light of Jesus pours in on a situation, the truth is unveiled.

Debauchery and doing evil comes from the depths of a person's heart. But many times it is propelled by an unforeseen foe, a menace creeping out of the dark unbeknown to man, except for the warnings from the book of a loving God. Peter warned, "Stay alert! Watch out for your great enemy, the devil. He prowls around like a roaring lion, looking for someone to devour" 1 Peter 5:8 (NLT).

Protective Armor

> "Finally, be strong in the Lord and in his mighty power. Put on the full armor of God so that you can take your stand against the devil's schemes." Ephesians 6:10-11

To be strong in the Lord and in His power is to depend on God to be your strength and to fight for you. Be aware that "the one who is in you [Holy Spirit] is greater than the one who is in the world [the devil]" 1 John 4:4. We deal with people with truth, mercy and compassion, but we deal with the devil with strength, not letting him have any space in our lives. The kingdom of God and the kingdom of darkness are two spiritual realms that coexist. Christians belong to God's kingdom, but the kingdom of darkness is still after us. So we have to get serious.

Paul wrote, "For our struggle is not against flesh and blood, but against the rulers, against the authorities, against the powers of this dark world and against the spiritual forces of evil in the heavenly realms" Ephesians 6:12. God gave us tools to conquer this unseen enemy. Armor was defensive coverings worn by men going into battle to give them protection from the attacks of their enemy. Putting on the full armor of God gives us protection from the attacks of our spiritual enemies. This is our protective covering from evil.

Paul said, "clothe yourself with the presence of the Lord Jesus Christ. And don't let yourself think about ways to indulge your evil desires" Romans 13:14 (NLT). The armor is a symbolic way of saying, "put on Christ." We put on the same wardrobe He wears. In otherwords, we clothe ourselves with His character.

In Ephesians 6 you will find all the parts of your spiritual armor listed. The armor of God includes truth, righteousness and the gospel of peace, plus the shield of faith, which extinguishes all the flaming arrows of the evil one. This shield of faith was a comparison to the large Roman shield, which was covered with leather, and then soaked in water to put out flame-tipped arrows. Additional armor includes salvation, the Word of God and prayer. Come to the place in your walk with the Lord where you can easily put on the full armor of God.

You do not have to be afraid of the enemy. When you stand against the devil and stand your ground, you are maintaining the position you have in Jesus Christ. The devil has no place in your life unless you give it to him. Founder of Touch of Fire Ministries, Bob Hazlett said, "Stop letting the devil put 'buts' in your way." We have everything we need to fight the devil and win, so stand firm against what he throws at you. Stand firm against his temptations to draw you away from serving God. Stand in the security of knowing the love that God has for you. James wrote, "Submit yourselves, then, to God. Resist the devil, and he will flee from you" James 4:7.

Sinking your teeth into His Word is food for your soul.

Do you have your armor on? Are you standing your ground with the armor of truth, righteousness, peace, faith, and salvation? Is God's Word deep in your heart? Sinking your teeth into His Word is food for your soul. Stay close to Him through prayer and depend on Him for His help.

The greatest threat to Satan is Jesus. It is by the Holy Spirit's power that you are growing up to be just like Him. He helps you live a life that pleases God. You can holler all you want at the enemy, but if you are not like Jesus, it won't even affect him. Pastor David Hess of Christ Community Church in Camp Hill, PA, said, "It's only a good fight if you win it. And God has placed you in the midst of a battle that He says you are going to win."

You can't always control the attacks, but you can win the battles. God has given you all the armor you need. Plus, His power is at work in you by the Holy Spirit. You do not have to be afraid of Satan's plans against you, because God has His own plans for you and His plans are good ones.

> "For I know the plans I have for you," declares the Lord, "plans to prosper you and not to harm you, plans to give you hope and a future."
> Jeremiah 29:11

As the football season was ending, it was the talk of the week. Teams aimed to be their best in order to make it to the highly esteemed Super Bowl. The defense players were at their peak. They were ready to resist any attack by their opponents, ready to protect and safeguard their team. Understanding that the one on the prowl plans to attack and defeat you, consider the readiness of those seasoned defense players. Are you at your peak of readiness? Are you ready to resist any attack by your enemy and opponent, ready to protect and safeguard your life with the armor of God?

Life's Struggles

"Call upon me in the day of trouble; I will deliver you," says the Lord in Psalm 50:15. Life can be tough, but the tough times are temporary. He takes those things meant to harm you and turns them around for good, to benefit you in some way. James wrote:

> "Consider it pure joy…whenever you face trials of many kinds, because you know that the testing of your faith develops perseverance. Perseverance must finish its work so that you may be mature and complete, not lacking anything." James 1:2-4

To "consider it pure joy" when you face problems didn't make any sense to me. I wanted to say, "Is he kidding?" Then I realized the joy was not because of the problem, but in spite of it. God wants to produce character in His children. Trying times gives character the opportunity to grow in us, bringing some meaning to our suffering. We can also be glad because we have someone greater than the problem to help us. God is on our side! Paul wrote:

> "We can rejoice, too, when we run into problems and trials, for we know that they help us develop endurance. And endurance develops strength of character, and character strengthens our confident hope of salvation. And this hope will not lead to disappointment. For we know how dearly God loves us, because he has given us the Holy Spirit

to fill our hearts with his love." Romans 5:3-5 (NLT)

Hope directs us towards our future resurrection, to an inheritance that is eternal. The goal of our faith is the salvation of our souls. Even though we may have trying times here, we have rewards waiting for us in heaven. Peter states, "In all this you greatly rejoice, though now for a little while you may have had to suffer grief in all kinds of trials" 1 Peter 1:6.

We would like everything to be wonderful all the time, but we recognize that isn't realistic. It even seems as if everything is going wrong sometimes. In those times more than ever, we need to remind ourselves that we can depend on God to be there for us. He will give us the strength we need to endure and conquer the trials of life. Problems force us to use our character muscles. We have the chance to use our faith to believe God rather than our circumstance. We can make decisions to choose His way in spite of difficulties. This makes us spiritually strong. It brings us into spiritual maturity.

It is now coming to my mind, all those people who have endured atrocious and unspeakable abuse, from little children to the elderly. Some suffering for years and even losing their lives at the hands of their abuser. How can these words that I write, these Scriptures that I quote, bring any kind of comfort to them? Will they seem useless and empty to such ones? Having just taught about the deception of Satan, is he now causing me to doubt that what I have written can help others? But God does not doubt the strength of His Word. He says, "my word that goes out from my mouth: It will not return to me empty, but will accomplish what I desire and achieve the purpose for which I sent it" Isaiah 55:11.

Twists and Turns

God brings hope, no matter how bad a situation is. Suffering does not last forever. For some, the misery ends as they walk into eternity surrounded and engulfed by a pure love they have never known, as Jesus their Savior greets them. Rescued survivors receive hope for a better future. If they haven't had the opportunity to receive salvation, that opportunity is now available to them. Life eternal with their Savior lies ahead, the final hope and their ultimate destiny.

Paul the apostle, the man who wrote many of the books in the New Testament, stresses that no trial is able to keep us from Jesus' love. "Who shall separate us from the love of Christ? Shall trouble or hardship or persecution or famine or nakedness or danger or sword?" Romans 8:35. Paul does not stop there, he continues: "For I am convinced that neither death nor life, neither angels nor demons, neither the present nor the future, nor any powers, neither height nor depth, nor anything else in all creation, will be able to separate us from the love of God that is in Christ Jesus our Lord" Romans 8:38-39. Look at some of his personal experiences:

> "Five times I received from the Jews the forty lashes minus one. Three times I was beaten with rods, once I was pelted with stones, three times I was shipwrecked, I spent a night and a day in the open sea, I have been constantly on the move. I have been in danger from rivers, in danger from bandits, in danger from my fellow Jews, in danger from Gentiles; in danger in the city, in danger in the country, in danger at sea; and in danger from false believers. I have labored and toiled and have often gone without sleep; I have known

hunger and thirst and have often gone without food; I have been cold and naked. Besides everything else, I face daily the pressure of my concern for all the churches." 2 Corinthians 11:24-28

Despite all this, he wrote, "Yet what we suffer now is nothing compared to the glory he will give us later" Romans 8:18 (TLB). James tells us, "Blessed is the one who perseveres under trial because, having stood the test, that person will receive the crown of life that the Lord has promised to those who love him" James 1:12. Satan tempts us to pull us down, hoping we will fail God's standards. God tests us to lift us up, to determine and sharpen our character.

> *Nothing can happen that you and God can't handle together.*

No matter what you go through, remember trying times will pass. Hard times are not here to stay. God has the ability to change the situation, but if He doesn't He gives you the strength to weather the storm. He will see you through. He is your strength and help in times of trouble. Nothing can happen that you and God can't handle together.

Bumps in the Road

Sometimes you have to hold on tight, because the road ahead may be bumpy and filled with potholes. Instead of shrinking back in fear, move forward with confidence in God. Hold on to Him and He will hold on to you. It may seem easier to give up or to give in at times, but don't give up and don't give in. It was written, "Since ancient times no one has heard, no ear has perceived, no eye has seen any God besides you, who acts on behalf of those who wait for him" Isaiah 64:4.

Life is a journey that takes you from one experience to another. Instead of a straight road, life is similar to a road filled with twists and turns. Curves wind *around* obstacles. Tunnels make their way *through* obstacles. Bridges go *over* obstacles. Bumps, hills and mountains greet you as you journey through life. God is with you in the beginning and will still be with you at the end. Look to Jesus as He takes you around, through and over the obstacles in your life. The Holy Spirit empowers you and sees you through it all.

My brother's love of flying led him to become a career pilot for a major airline. I asked him how he handled air pockets that cause a plane to drop for a few seconds before leveling out again. This dropping sensation causes fear, anxiety and feelings of helplessness in many of the passengers. He replied, "When we hit air pockets, I think of them as bumps in a road."

I have experienced the bumps that come along in life and you will experience bumps in your life, we all do. My question to you is this, "As problems arise in your life, do you view them with fear, worry or helplessness or as another bump in the road on the way to your destination?"

Chapter 6

A Pity Party

There was a time when I focused on all the problems and trouble in my life. I dismissed the joy that comes from knowing God and who I am in Him. Instead, I held pity parties and concentrated on my own misery. As a result, I was always miserable. "Woe is me" became my signature phrase.

One day my young son said to me, "Mom, all you ever say is, 'Woe is me' and I'm tired of hearing it." Listening to him repeat it made me realize how it really sounded. I was also reinforcing the negative things in my life when I spoke that way. At that very moment I decided my life would change and "woe is me" would no longer be part of my vocabulary. I can gratefully announce that my life did begin changing for the better, but it was a process, one that required a brand new attitude on my part in order to begin. That change in attitude involved giving God my past and trusting Him with my future.

One of the important things I learned is that my past did not have to destroy my future. Your past does not have to destroy yours either. What you do today and in the future is what is important now. So it is not necessary to drag your past failures and hurtful memories into today and into tomorrow.

Dale Flynn wrote, "What a world this would be if we could forget our troubles as easily as we forget our blessings."[1]

God frequently uses other people in our life to bring us comfort and encouragement. Paul wrote this about his experience:

> But God, who comforts the downcast, comforted us by the coming of Titus, and not only by his coming but also by the comfort you had given him. He told us about your longing for me, your deep sorrow, your ardent concern for me, so that my joy was greater than ever." 2 Corinthians 7:6-7

Sweeten the bumps in your life by using them to develop compassion for those who are hurting and to help others going through similar situations. Paul wrote, "Therefore encourage one another and build each other up" 1 Thessalonians 5:11. Knowing you made it through and have come out on the other side becomes hope and reassurance for others. In like manner, friends you trust are able to support and encourage you.

Although we all need others in our lives, no greater love than God's exist. Change worry into reliance on Him. Healing and peace come as you lean on Him. Being stuck in the past will only hold you back. It is time to move forward with new life. Out with the old and in with the new!

Slip Ups

Even though problems and trials are a part of this life, I resist accepting that fact. I do not like the stress, the negative thoughts or distressing feelings that come with trying times. But I have decided that instead of being surprised every time a bad situation comes my way, I will remember it is an opportunity to solve a dilemma and trust God for His assistance. Instead of becoming weaker or broken, I will become stronger and wiser because of them.

If we make a mistake or encounter failure, we can look at it in the context of a problem that needs solved or overcome. Knowledge gained from our mistakes, enables us to look for better ways. A friend wisely said, "We all make mistakes in life, and learn from both the good and bad choices we make." Yet fear of failure can repeatedly keep a person from stepping out. Obtaining success requires patience and the fortitude to continue trying. We just have to hang in there and not be so quick to give up!

The basketball player LeBron James said, "You have to accept failure to get better." Failure or mistakes can lead to future triumphs. A failure or a mistake is an action—not an identity. When you slip up, it means you are human. You can always recover and you can start your day over anytime. It is written, "Great is his faithfulness; his loving-kindness begins afresh each day" Lamentations 3:23 (TLB).

The teacher of this little boy called him slow and too stupid to learn. All he had was three months of schooling. But his mother refused to be discouraged and taught him herself at home. By the age of ten, he was reading on a college level and had built a chemistry lab in his basement. There, he had thousands of failures before perfecting his invention—the light bulb! Thomas Edison went on to create and develop over 1300 inventions and eventually held 1093 patents. However, two success stories are found here: a boy willing to learn even when faced with overwhelming difficulties and a mother who would not give up.

This man's love for writing motivated him to write a series of fairy tales. Unfortunately, they just did not sell. He finally landed a job with a newspaper. The paper's editor fired him not too long after he started the job. His boss claimed he did not have any good ideas to contribute and had a habit of doodling too much. The editor also did not hesitate to tell him that he didn't have any talent. But in the end, it was Walt Disney's "doodling" that led to the creation of Mickey Mouse, Donald Duck, Goofy, Pluto and all the gang! He went on to build the most famous theme parks in the world—Disneyland and Walt Disney World. Even more astounding, he won worldwide acclaim and was the winner of forty-five academy awards.

These are just a few of the famous people in history who did not let failure stop them. In fact, they went on to turn their failure into success. What did these people have in common?

- They had an idea, a goal or a vision.
- They took chances again and again.
- They were people who didn't give up.
- They made mistakes, but they learned from them.
- They took their failures in stride and kept on trying.

Have you set goals to propel yourself forward? Do you have clearly defined, specific short-term and long-term goals written down? Are they mapped out in detail, providing steps to implement along the way to get you there? Be careful not to let the fear of failure prevent you from achieving. You have to take chances in order to find success. In other words, you are never defeated if you never stop trying.

Some people think God won't use them or is not pleased with them, because of problems in their lives, or because of mistakes or wrong choices they made. Be assured, it is a fact that He uses imperfect people. The truth is we all have flaws. Besides, if He used only perfect people, where would He find them? Your inability to do everything perfect does not make you a failure. You could be doing even better than you think. Yet, if you still think you do not measure up, let Him make up the difference. Paul said, "I can do all this through him who gives me strength" Philippians 4:13.

Troubles

I often hear the following Scripture used when someone is going through a very difficult time, and they feel as though they cannot take anymore. It is as if this verse should encourage them: "No temptation has overtaken you except what is common to mankind. And God is faithful; he will not let you be tempted beyond what you can bear. But when you are tempted, he will also provide a way out so that you can endure it" 1 Corinthians 10:13. Some people translate this Scripture to mean that God won't allow us to endure more trouble or pain than we can bear, than we are able to handle. This is an example of what happens when Scripture is taken out of context. "Temptation" refers to anything that draws us into sin.

In this chapter, Paul is talking to Christians in the town of Corinth about the history of the Israelites who God brought out of slavery in Egypt. Instead of being thankful, and honoring and trusting God because of everything He had done for them, these people sinned by following the traditions of those around them. They had joined in their idol worship and pagan immorality. The temptations of the society and culture around the Israelites of old drew them into sin.

Paul reminded the new Christians in his day, who were coming out of a similar society, that this behavior did not please God. He also told them they should not be sinning, grumbling and testing God as those people had. These things were recorded to be an example for us too. We don't want to find ourselves following the ways of those around us, if those ways oppose God's righteous standards.

This chapter also tells us that God enables us to stand up to or resist temptations. But if a person doesn't follow the promptings of the Holy Spirit and gives in to the temptation, then it becomes sin. James wrote, "When tempted, no one should say, 'God is tempting me.' For God cannot be tempted by evil, nor does he tempt anyone; but each person is tempted when they are dragged away by their own evil desire and enticed" James 1:13-14.

Although God's very nature is love, have you still wondered, "If God loves me so much, why do I go through such bad times?" Be assured the unpleasant or hurtful times you encounter are not what He desires for you as His child. They are not His best for you. James said, "Don't be deceived, my dear brothers and sisters. Every good and perfect gift is from above, coming down from the Father of the heavenly lights, who does not change like shifting shadows" James 1:16-17. Matthew said, "If you, then, though you are evil, know how to give good gifts to your children, how much more will your Father in heaven give good gifts to those who ask him!" Matthew 7:11. This is your heavenly Father's desire for you. He longs to fill your life with good things, with His blessings.

A Pity Party

Troublesome times can plague our lives because of wrong actions performed by others, from accidents or natural disasters. Sometimes they come because of wrong decisions we made, or because of things we did that we should not have done, or maybe because of things we should have done and did not do. And of course, sometimes things just happen. However, because of God's goodness and our love for Him, He will find a way to use these situations to give us a positive ray of sunshine. I call this particular Scripture the one where God takes lemons and makes lemonade: "And we know that in all things God works for the good of those who love him, who have been called according to his purpose" Romans 8:28.

Situations meant for our harm will become God's tool to develop character in us that is more like His Son's. Undesirable, unwanted situations that arrive in our lives may also give us an opportunity to assist or encourage others. Adverse situations may even cause us to discover things about ourselves we were not aware of, and then we are able to modify or improve our behavior. Other times we get to practice patience or extend mercy.

I sat in one of the many look-alike reclining chairs in the sterilized white room, with my back to the sunshine pouring in through a large window. Lined up on both sides of me were others relaxing in their chairs, all with IV's attached to veins in their arms or in ports attached to veins in their chests. I looked around at this sight. Some slept, others read, a few stared into space, while others munched on snacks. For eight months I witnessed this scene, as caring nurses and doctors watched over their patients.

Earlier I had asked myself, "Which is the worse of the two evils, treatment or no treatment?" My decision was to accept the chemo treatment. What useful purpose could I find in my situation now, as chemo medicines dripped into my body? I didn't dwell on the harm and destruction it was also doing, since the chemo treatment of today attacks both the well-functioning and faulty cells.

I was looking for a purpose beyond the assistance the chemotherapy would give my body to eradicate the cancer. In the midst of it, I found the opportunity. On the days I spent time in the treatment room, I would pray for each patient there. Occasionally my appointments would coincide with some of the same people, and I looked forward to our small chats. Acquiring more information about their individual sickness and needs, made it possible for me to pray for them in more detail. Sending prayers up on their behalf became my opportunity and ray of sunshine.

Looking for Love

Some people think God is too far away to care about their situation. But He isn't distant, uncaring or unknowing. He wants everyone to know His love. His heart cries out for His people. He is waiting for them to believe Him. He is not a fleeting thought or an unknown god; His glory and majesty shines through His creation.

One afternoon as I was reading the Bible, God's love was so impressed on my heart that I thought, "Everyone needs to know the depth of His love for us." The next moment I was given the opportunity to experience His love in a tangible way. I can only describe it as a very unique feeling. It was as if liquid love was raining down, pouring over me from heaven. Since I was little, I had sung the song "Jesus Loves Me," so I knew He loved me. Now I wanted to make sure others knew how great His love was.

A Pity Party

If you have felt unlovable, unworthy or unwanted, you may think there is no way God could care about you, let alone love you or help you. We may have moments when such thoughts cross our minds, but that is not the way the Lord feels about us. One day as I was flipping through a pile of old papers, I came across a sheet with those exact words written across the top. In large letters it said, "I feel unlovable, unworthy and unwanted." I looked at my list in shock. At the time I experienced His liquid love, I thought it was so I could tell others. All along, He had been ministering to me too, ministering to those deep places of hurt in my heart. Those places that we often try to hide even from ourselves. "The heart is deceitful above all things" Jeremiah 17:9.

The God of this universe loves you, delights in you, wants you, accepts you and has a purpose for your life. His banner over you is truly love despite adverse times that arise now and then. Can you comprehend this fact? He has taken you from the kingdom of darkness and set you in His kingdom of light. He has taken you from death and given you eternal life. Did you also know He calls you by name; He knows the number of hairs on your head; and He carries your picture in His Hand?

Jesus came to set us free from all the burdens that weigh us down, but we are so busy running here and there, we frequently don't take the time to sit and talk with Him. Yet, He is so full of love for us. When will we value how much He loves us? Everything He does is for the benefit of His people.

The Word of God reveals His desire to bless you, offering to you peace, joy, strength and many more blessings. Turn toward Him, so He can bring you out of your life of burdens and trials and set you in a new realm of peace and happiness.

Enjoy the love He has for you, and soon words and songs of praise will automatically escape from your lips.

You may remember the country song, "Looking for Love in all the Wrong Places." Many people tend to look to others for the unconditional love only God can give. Then they wonder why they are always disappointed. Your worth is not found in how someone else thinks of you or even how you may think of yourself. Find it in how God thinks about you. Have you been waiting for someone to make you feel valuable, worthy and lovable? God will! I heard the Lord say:

> "Come here beside Me, close to Me. Hear what I have to say. I have come that you have life and life more abundantly. Freedom is what I bring; freedom from sin and freedom to live. See, I bring life; not pain, not suffering.
>
> Jump for joy and expect more. I am a giver and my love I give to you. It is my life. I am the One who loves you, the One who cares. Hear Me with your heart. Hold unto Me and never let go. I am your strength. I am your joy. I am all you need."

Carry On

Life is full of wonderful, tender and ecstatic moments: being in love, watching a colorful sunset, listening to the sound of waves licking at the sandy beach, experiencing a beautiful wedding, watching a little one take his first step, catching your first fish, winning the golf game... However, life doesn't stop there. It is also full of pain, illness, shock, hurt, rejection, offense and a conglomeration of other negative emotions and events.

There seems to be just as many reactions to harmful or discouraging life events. Some people say, "So what, that's life," and move on. Others succumb to the weight of it all and withdraw from life. Others continue filled with bitterness and resentment. Some hide the pain in the depth of their hearts. Still others have hearts covered with so many scars there isn't room for more.

I have never liked the words "get over it." Some people say, "Everyone gets hurt now and then—so get over it." Perhaps. Perhaps not. In addition, there is nothing encouraging about that statement. It is easy for others to say, because they did not experience or endure the pain that left scars on the suffering person's mind and heart. We should never trivialize a person's pain or problem, no matter how insignificant it may seem to us. Their problems can be discouraging, hurtful or crushing, just as your problems can be to you. I have even witnessed a person blaming problems on hormones. Fluctuating hormones may intensify feelings, but they do not create problems. Problems need addressed and solutions found.

It is a struggle for many people to let go of the wrongs done and abuse endured. I wonder how many aches and pains are festering behind scabs and scars on the body or in the heart? How much is hiding in the hidden recesses of the mind in an attempt to appear normal, or behind the emotionless face that conveys, "I don't have a care in the world"?

God's word instructs us to comfort, encourage and support each other. However, when we aren't sure what to say, we have to be careful not to over-simplify or over-spiritualize by using old stand-bys. Other comments used: have more faith, confess the Word, put it behind you, grow up, etc. Maybe you can think of other remarks that are over-used. Hurting people do not need bombarded with clichés, even if they are Christian clichés.

The tragedy is some people face such devastating and life-threatening hardships that they could state with Paul and his team, "We were really crushed and overwhelmed, and feared we would never live through it." Nevertheless, Paul continued:

> "We felt we were doomed to die and saw how powerless we were to help ourselves; but that was good, for then we put everything into the hands of God, who alone could save us, for he can even raise the dead. And he did help us and saved us from a terrible death; yes, and we expect him to do it again and again. But you must help us too by praying for us. For much thanks and praise will go to God from you who see his wonderful answers to your prayers for our safety!" 2 Corinthians 1:8-11 (TLB)

In Paul's example, we see an important action that we can take to help others. Our prayers make a difference, not only in our own lives, but also in the lives of others. James wrote, "The prayer of a righteous person is powerful and effective" James 5:16.

The seesaw I played on as a young child comes to mind: sometimes we are up, sometimes we are down. When we are down, we need our victorious friends to stand with us. When they are down, we become their victorious friends to cheer them on. When people are hurting, more often than not, they need compassion, a reason to hope and a listening ear. Being a good listener is better than doing a lot of talking. Just showing up to be close, shows we care.

Staying stuck in despair is not living. Acknowledging your pain helps you face it and begin to heal. Sometimes you just need to rest. If you are in such a period, take that needed time to rest with your caring, loving heavenly Father. He is a strong and mighty God. Rest in Him and see what He will do. He says, "Come to me, all you who are weary and burdened, and I will give you rest" Matthew 11:28.

Even though it is easy to feel weakened by troubling situations, the Lord will strengthen you. The Psalmist wrote,

> "God is our refuge and strength,
> an ever-present help in trouble.
> Therefore we will not fear, though the earth give way
> and the mountains fall into the heart of the sea,
> though its waters roar and foam
> and the mountains quake with their surging."
> Psalm 46:1-3

When I was feeling the effects of the chemotherapy draining the life from me, sapping the energy from my muscles, the sight from my eyes, the sharpness from my mind, I asked God, "Where are You?" He answered, "See, I am with you. I haven't left you. I am still here. I see all and I know all. Continue to believe in Me and trust in Me. You will not be disappointed." And I wasn't disappointed. He will walk through our worst situations with us.

Use both the good and the bad experiences as opportunities to build both good and godly character, to commune with the God who cares about you and loves you, to right wrongs, to fix weaknesses and to rest in God's strength. During the trying times, look forward with hope to a better day. Now it is time to carry on.

On His Heart

I remember the time when I wished God still spoke to us today as He did in the Old Testament times. David wrote, "My heart has heard you say, "Come and talk with me." And my heart responds, "Lord, I am coming" Psalm 27:8 (NLT).

God's desire from the beginning was to talk with us. He spoke with Adam and Eve in the garden and with many others, as described for us throughout the Old Testament. Over the years, God used many methods to reveal Himself. He spoke with Abraham face to face. He spoke through dreams and revealed the interpretation of dreams to Joseph. Moses heard an audible voice. Mary received a message from God when He sent the archangel Gabriel to her. Jesus personally appeared to Paul in His glorified body.

I questioned, "If He spoke then, why not to us now?" In Hebrews 13:8, we read, "Jesus Christ is the same yesterday and today and forever." Then I came across the Scripture that states His people will know His voice. In the following Scriptures, Jesus refers to Himself as the shepherd and He refers to His people as His sheep: "I am the good shepherd; I know my sheep and my sheep know me...My sheep listen to my voice; I know them, and they follow me" John 10:14, 27.

I discovered it was true; He does speak to us today—if we would only listen. He has many ways He communicates with us: through His Word in the Bible, by teachers and preachers of His Word, sometimes through a friend or even a stranger. He may speak to us during our prayer time. He may also use visions or dreams to communicate with us or to get our attention. Others hear from the Lord through a prophecy given to them. Many people hear a still, small voice speaking to their hearts, or an impression or feeling of something God wants them to do. Also know that He will never speak anything that contradicts His Word.

So don't turn a deaf ear and say He doesn't speak. He wants to reveal Himself to you as the God who loves you. The more time you spend with Him, the more you will come to know Him. He desires to carry your cares, lift your burdens and heal your broken heart. Rejoice in His goodness. Walk with Him and talk with Him. You are forever on His heart and mind. When God calls you to come and talk with Him, to visit with Him a little while, do you respond as David did? Do you say, "Lord, I am coming"?

Chapter 7

Wounds of the Heart

"Give it to the Lord." With these words, we want to encourage someone who is hurting or who has been offended. We are familiar with Scriptures that tell us we can take our cares and our burdens to the Lord, and He will help us. This sounds good, makes sense and seems to be the right thing to say. Occasionally, when we discuss problems with trusted friends to relieve the stress building up inside, it may bring relief for only a short time. Even our discussions with the Lord may end with this same result. If the memories and the pain come back without mercy, refreshed and ready for another round in the unending sea of circulating memories, take them back to the Lord and then continue the process of forgiving.

This teaching—give it to God and leave it with Him—can be compared to a young child taking his trouble to his father, then trusting him to take care of the situation for him. Giving God our cares does not mean acting as if they never happened. It does mean we trust Him to help us. When I discern I'm in a situation that I have no control over, I look to God and rely on Him to handle it and work it out for me. If He tells me not to intervene in a situation, I have to depend on Him and stay out of it. Otherwise, I look to Him to come beside me to find a solution.

The mention or discussion of negative events in one's life doesn't mean unforgiveness is being harbored. Forgiving a situation, giving it to the Lord or leaving it with Him, doesn't cancel it from a person's memory banks. What it does do is provide relief from the hurt, and release from the control that situation or offending person had over one's mind. So of course, life events come up in conversation. It may mean only that a person is relating what was witnessed or experienced—human nature hampered by the evil one or by an uncaring, unloving heart.

Very often, false beliefs become lingering symptoms of long ago hurts. These beliefs or lies accepted as truth become part of our daily living by influencing our thinking, actions and how we view the world, even how we relate to God.

Have lies settled in your heart, making you think you are:

o   unworthy
o   unlovable
o   a bad person
o   not good enough
o   unable to do anything right
o   incapable of making a good decision

Do the lies you have believed make you feel:

o   incompetent
o   inadequate
o   incapable

Do false beliefs tell you that you:

- have no voice
- are worthless
- shouldn't exist
- are a bother

Is it possible your negative beliefs aren't serving you? Go from the negative thought to the turn-around phrase, "I wonder if it's possible that..." Insert a statement that applies to you. For instance, go from the belief, "I am incapable" to "I wonder if it's possible that I am capable." Carry through to the positive statement, "I am capable." Work through this until you can feel it is real or true, moving away from the destructive belief.

To identify where a harmful belief comes from, reach into the past to reveal the root cause—when the lie was first planted. It is not necessary to examine each thought or memory for healing. Search for the root lie, and then apply the truth. For example, change the lie that says, "I am unlovable" to the truth, which says, "I am loveable." Then everything related gets knocked down, as dominos set in a line.

The many lies planted in a young child's life can change their course forever. Even what appears to be the most innocent of situations to an adult can cause little ones, with young developing minds, to believe lies about themselves, causing them to become people pleasers, unable to make decisions, afraid to set boundaries, afraid to say no and the list could go on. God would like us to be free from all those hindrances.

Our emotions flow from what we believe. We feel what we accept as true. We live what we feel. Becoming aware of God's presence and His truth in those situations will begin to eradicate false beliefs—the lies that were unknowingly instilled in one's heart. Acknowledging and stating His truth silence lies and related emotions. What He has to say, overrides the harmful words and actions of others. It is time to decide that what God thinks is more important. Your earthly parents may not have been perfect, but your heavenly Father is. Jesus did not bring a message of condemnation, but one of love. John wrote, "God did not send his Son into the world to condemn the world, but to save the world through him" John 3:17.

Healing takes time. No one else can comprehend the depth of your hurt except God. A broken heart discolored from wounds and scars takes time to heal. Acknowledge flashbacks, but then come back to today and continue moving forward into a new day.

Consider the benefit a counselor can have in helping you walk through hurtful memories. Trained Christian counselors can lead to the truth about a situation, dispelling any lies instilled. Check with your church. They may know of an inner healing ministry in your area to assist your walk through wounded areas of your life. In the book *Safe People*, it says, "Finally, we use the community for wisdom and knowledge....Often we are too caught up in the problem to see things objectively....And they can offer wise counsel to us as well as to the person with whom we are struggling."[1]

Healing includes breaking the lies instilled, possibly over years. Dismantling the lies that controlled you leads to healing. It's about accepting God's truth. Once the truth is accepted, the lie is defeated and loses its control. It can't play havoc with your thoughts and emotions any more. When the agreement with the lie is broken, truth brings order and peace ensues.

The Little Girl

She was only four. Her newest feat was putting the record on her red and white square player. Grasping the swinging arm of the player, she carefully set the needle on the record. Her favorite song about the bear began to play. She loved to sing along as the record spun around creating lively music. And she would dance and dance. Her mother glimpsed the little girl's joy. She praised and encouraged her to sing and dance even more, adding, "When your father comes home from work, you can play your favorite song and sing and dance for him too."

He pulled up a chair and waited while she prepared the record. With great happiness, the little girl twirled and sang. She had practiced all afternoon so she could do her very best. As her favorite song ended, her father turned to her mother with a stone-faced look. "Is that it? Is this what you wanted me to see?" Getting up from his chair, he walked away without a word to the waiting, expectant little girl.

The feelings of rejection, unappreciated and unworthy of his praise and delight were new to her, as they swirled and rushed through her hurting heart. She had expected her father to be pleased; instead, she found herself surprised and confused. Sadness overcame her. Her head hung low as she gazed at the floor feeling so alone. "What just happened?" Her young mind was still trying to make sense of the turmoil and sadness she felt. The little girl decided that she wasn't good enough. In reality, her father didn't know how to relate or respond to this little dancing top before him. He had grown up in a house full of rough and tumbling boys. Unknown to the little girl, a figure of a strong, solid man stood cattycornered to where she stood as though glued to the floor.

Years later, her thoughts take her back in time to the scene that left her scarred. The same manly figure appears and shows her a different outcome. He wants to make his presence known to the brokenhearted little girl, who now lives in a woman's body. She watched the scene play before her: the little girl looking after her father as he walks away.

The man hidden from her sight now calmly approaches and lifts her head. As her eyes meet his gaze, she feels his love and acceptance. A smile broadens across his face. He had been watching the whole time. He was delighted with her song and dance. Bending down he took his strong comforting arms and wrapped them around her, giving her the biggest, longest, most loving hug she ever felt. It was as if she was being snuggled in a soft, warm blanket.

She had grown up with the feeling of rejection haunting her. She thought she always had to try harder to be accepted. She learned it was needful to please others in order to be accepted and loved. Believing those lies, the little girl made an agreement to accept rejection, because no matter how hard she tried, her best never seemed good enough.

Finally, she recognizes the truth. She saw Him with her own eyes. He was there all along, delighting in her, accepting her, loving her and enjoying her song. The lies cannot stay, as she breaks her agreement with them. She doesn't have to live with rejection any longer. Instead, she will always know that she pleases and is accepted by the Lord.

He was There

The young child looked upon a horrible scene. She stood shocked, unable to move. "It has to stop," she thought, afraid to intervene. Hurrying for help she said, "Come and see."

The words to express what was happening would not come. Help arrived, but the scene had stopped. It became a memory that occasionally still haunted her. Looking back in time the question was asked, "Jesus where were you then? Show me." Only she could not see Him. She waited. She still was unable to sense His presence.

We may feel alone at times, yet we are never truly alone. Becky Hunter wrote, "So whether I'm taking in the majestic or the superfluous I can almost always find Him. And when He's nowhere to be found, I know the problem is my limited sight, not His disappearance."[2]

Once again, thinking about the scene from so long ago, it came to her that she did not want Jesus there. She didn't want Him to witness what was taking place. The Lord should not see such things. No longer that young child, she realizes He has witnessed much worse brutality in this world starved of love. Looking back, she asked Him again to show her His presence in this scene.

In her mind's eye, she saw the young girl as she stood watching, unable to intervene, unable to stop it. Feelings of being incapable and weak rushed over her. She turned to see Jesus kneeling behind her. She hid her frightened face in His shoulder, not wanting to see the scene before her. He was looking. He was watching. He embraced her and then gave her the strength to go for help.

The Lord had been with her even then. She now understood. She was not responsible for what she saw happening; He was there to carry the burden. She was not responsible for carrying the pain of others; Jesus does that. She was not responsible for hiding what occurred; the one wounding was responsible for the consequences of his actions. She accepted the truth. At last, the agreements with the lies of being weak and incapable were broken. With the Lord by her side, she would always be strong, having His strength to draw on.

A Special Creation

In the beginning, God started humanity with Adam and Eve, making them in His image and likeness. Young children often express the desire to grow up to be like their mom or dad. In a similar manner, our greatest aspiration should be to be like our heavenly Father—wise, kind, merciful, patient and loving. We copy other characteristics from Him as well, like decision-making, designing, inventing and creating.

When the first couple choose to rebel against His authority, a sin nature was set in motion and it became our inheritance too. This nature pulls us into negative behaviors, which includes selfishness, jealousy and rebellion. We can stop the pull of this sin nature in its tracks. Reverse it by accepting all that Jesus did for us, embracing God's way of doing things and letting the Holy Spirit help us. Now once again the desire to be like our heavenly Father will be our first aspiration.

The Holy Spirit helps you make right decisions and choices. It is not something you have to do by yourself or struggle to do. This is another display of God's loving-kindness. You are His special creation and no other person is exactly like you. He sees, hears, notices, remembers and loves you.

Live in grace and emotional wholeness by uncovering the lies you have accepted as true, and subject them to the truth of God. Allow Jesus to come into your inner sanctuary, where your mind and heart meet, and wash away the lies planted knowingly or unknowingly in your life. His light shines and brings truth and healing to those festering wounds deep within. His love surrounds you. Have you felt, experienced and absorbed His love?

Waves of Life

The waves of life carry us here and there. They may carry us out into the glassy, calm sea. They may throw us around as they rise and fall. They could slap us against a rock or tumble us across the sand. They can lick our ankles or push us along in the surf to shore. Who knows where the waves of life might take us.

In the midst of the tumbling, the Lord waits for you to come to Him. He is there with you, so lean on Him. He will never withdraw His love from you. He is not blind that He cannot see or deaf that He cannot hear all that goes on in the lives of those who love Him. He draws you with His love, a love that is never ending and never burdensome. You will see prayers answered and desires met, as you spend time with Him. The Psalmist wrote:

The heartaches of this world are temporary, but His love is eternal.

> "Trust in the LORD and do good;
> dwell in the land and enjoy safe pasture.
> Take delight in the LORD,
> and he will give you the desires of your heart."
> Psalm 37:3-4

All good things are found in His presence, because He is good. He has blessings waiting for us. Paul wrote of God's desire to use His power to bless us: "Now to him who is able to do immeasurably more than all we ask or imagine, according to his power that is at work within us" Ephesians 3:20.

The Lord longs to show you all that He is. The heartaches of this world are temporary, but His love is eternal. There is a better time coming. It is time to prepare for the return of Jesus. He came to save the world, and now it is in need of His intervention once again.

> "For to us a child is born, to us a son is given, and the government will be on his shoulders. And he will be called Wonderful Counselor, Mighty God, Everlasting Father, Prince of Peace. Of the greatness of his government and peace there will be no end." Isaiah 9:6-7

Times are changing and His time is coming. It may be closer than we think. The clock is ticking. I believe the race is on and we are in the homestretch. So make ready; prepare to meet your King. It is time for rejoicing. The opportunity is coming to know Him as He is in all His glory. I heard the Lord say:

> "The time is growing short. All things must come to an end. Old things pass away that the new and glorious may spring forth. What you look for, what you pray for is about to happen. It is on the horizon. My Son stands ready to return. His steed paws the air, the angels shout, the warring angels stand ready to receive their orders."

You will have the opportunity to experience Him as He is and He will wrap His love around you. In His presence is joy forever more. So don't sink in despair, instead lift your head up and look to Him. Sing praises to Him in thanksgiving. Go to Him and be at peace. Experience His glory and His joy. It doesn't matter what comes your way, He will love you and be with you. David wrote, "The Lord is my strength and my shield; my heart trusts in him, and he helps me. My heart leaps for joy, and with my song I praise him" Psalm 28:7.

Stressing Out

Are you stressed and need comfort or just a time of rest? Go to your God, your heavenly Father. He will hold you and comfort you. You are His daughter. You are His son. Rejoice in Him. Even though life is short, you will have Him for eternity, in that you can rejoice. Go to His secret place through prayer and stay a while with Him. In your busyness, are you too quick to leave? Enjoy resting in His presence. It is a safe haven for you. So go and be with Him.

It is easy to become burdened down with the cares of this world. But 1 Peter 5:7 says, "Cast all your anxiety on him because he cares for you." Cast means to throw off or away, to get rid of or to discard. When you discard something, you do not get it back. After giving your worry or problem to the Lord, allow Him to keep the stress that came with it and be open to His help. Even our money has printed on it, "In God we trust." Yet from time to time, it seems we do everything to leave Him out of our lives.

Faith in good things happening isn't the answer. Faith in in others or even in ourselves isn't always helpful, but faith in God is. It is based on His character and His truth, and not on our emotions. He is our comforter and help in times of trouble. However, Some people would rather throw tantrums and cry, whine and shake their fists at God when things don't go the way they think they should. I heard the Lord ask, "How long will they turn their backs on me or blame me for all their troubles, when my desire is to bless them?"

When we give our most impossible or hurtful situations to Him, we can still be left with a turmoil of emotions, as well as feeling indecisive or hopeless. These emotions tend to continue to plague us, because we still need the solution or an answer. We may need boldness to say or do what we need to. We may still need strength to get through it or strength not to give up. We may need hope for the future or the ability and desire to go on. These are the exact things we can expect God to assist us with if we ask Him. He is not just a sounding board to land our frustrations on; He is our "help." His timetable is often different from ours, so we have to be careful to remain patient and to continue trusting Him while we wait.

One time, He answered a prayer for me, but only partially. I asked Him why He granted only part of my request. I heard Him say that I needed to be more specific when I prayed. So be specific in your requests when looking to Him for answers, for solutions, for boldness or for whatever your needs are. Realize how much He cares about you and wants to help you. As you expect and receive answers, your trust in Him will continue to grow. You will see, He does care and is closer than you thought.

Focusing on life's problems or on problems you think might pop up only drains your energy. Instead, make the Lord and His might the focus of your life. PJ of Signs and Wonders, Inc. wrote, "Ever had a problem that tried to take all your focus? God does not want any problem to take more than a glance from us. He wants our focus to remain on His promises....if we're secure in the Word of God, no problem is hopeless."[3]

If you have questions seek God, He has your answers. Understand how much He wants to do for you. Understand how much He loves you. Most important, He offers forgiveness, redemption, a new life and eternity with Him. John wrote, "We love because he first loved us" 1 John 4:19. Know Him as the Father who loves you and wants to care for you. Make this a new day as you rejoice in Him. I pray that His love covers you, His blessings overflow in your life and you experience all He has to offer.

And now, walk with Him—not behind Him, not ahead of Him, but beside Him. Do not waver; hold on to His hand. He will be your strength. Absorb His healing balm as He pours it out, reaching into those deep wells of hurt. Rejoice in God and go with Him into this new day. "Let the peace of Christ rule in your hearts, since as members of one body you were called to peace. And be thankful" Colossians 3:15. Take your praises to the Lord and set the world on fire with His Word. The Lord will bring in peace; the peace the world longs for.

Chapter 8

Bemoaning the Times

My granddaughter was bemoaning the state the world was in. Everything negative and evil you read or hear in the news was bothering her sensitive heart. Unfortunately, evil has been with the world for a very long time. Looking back at least six thousand years, the Bible and history records wars and multitudes of terrible events that took place in past societies. Today, lives filled with trouble, heartache and sorrow continues.

"It was better in your day," my granddaughter finally said. "I wish it was like it was in my grandparents' day."

In response to his daughter's statement, her father said, "Change it."

"Say something positive," her mother added.

What good answers. What better way to combat wrong than to change it by doing what is right and doing what we can to make a difference for the better. Ephesians 2:10 tells us, "We are God's handiwork, created in Christ Jesus to do good works." Writer Carolyn Shockey of New Port Richey, Florida wrote: "Today, with its technology and resources, more "ordinary folks" have the ability to reach many more people outside their inner circles, so the ability to impact others is much larger. Yet...be satisfied with making a difference by living a life of example, selflessness, love and compassion for others, assured that we have lit a candle in our corner of the world, lighting the way for others who follow us."[1]

Becoming lax and uncaring about the troubles of today isn't helpful. A verse in Proverbs says, "The prudent see danger and take refuge, but the simple keep going and pay the penalty" Proverbs 22:3. We should be concerned with what is happening in our world today. We shouldn't be indifferent or have an "I don't care" attitude. Yet, if we become overly worried about anything, it is possible to fall into bouts of anxiety, bringing us to a standstill instead of motivating us to move forward.

It's difficult to enjoy life when anxiety becomes dominate. God realizes how worried we can become. He gave us the antidote by telling us to put all our anxiety, all our cares on Him, allowing us to be more relaxed instead of uptight and overly stressed. This is where prayer comes in. We can pray: pray for each other, our friends, neighbors, leaders, our country, towns and cities.

If we continue to dwell on everything that is wrong, it will soon pull us down making us feel helpless and hopeless. Paul tells us to think on these things: "Finally, brothers and sisters, whatever is true, whatever is noble, whatever is right, whatever is pure, whatever is lovely, whatever is admirable—if anything is excellent or praiseworthy—think about such things" Philippians 4:8. The Word tells us to think on pleasant and good things for a reason; they bring hope and possibilities.

If I find myself complaining or becoming negative, I try to follow up with some positive thoughts and statements. Which is easier to say while getting up in the morning, "I hope this isn't going to be another miserable day" or "This is the day the Lord has made, and I'm going to rejoice and be glad in it"? If you think about it, it doesn't take any more time to be positive than to be negative. So why not spend your time being positive. When you have negative thoughts the tendency is to dwell on them, which is unproductive. Positive thoughts lead to action and satisfaction. Do you hear the Lord saying,

> "Don't give up. Don't get so overwhelmed with this life and all that you see that goes on in the world. Live your life walking by my side. Then contentment and happiness won't slip through your fingers. All my blessings will explode in your life."

Our purpose is to be a light shining in the darkness. That light comes from God living His life through us. By living His Word and being His representative of righteousness, we fill our little part of the world with His glory. You are one, then another is added and another. Soon, many people are seeking truth and living His way. Goodness shines a light in the darkness. As His love flows into our hearts, it will also flow out. Love is the centerpiece. Love can grow and expand in this way until it encompasses the entire world.

It doesn't take any more time to be positive, than to be negative.

> "You are the light of the world. A town built on a hill cannot be hidden....In the same way,

let your light shine before others, that they may see your good deeds and glorify your Father in heaven." Matthew 5:14, 16

Request Granted

I often wondered about the woman who Jesus initially ignored and then indicated He wouldn't help. I thought, "Wasn't that a mean thing for Him to do? And wasn't His analogy degrading to her?" Even before indicating He wouldn't help her, He refused to answer her until His disciples finally intervened.

> "Jesus then left that part of the country and walked the fifty miles to Tyre and Sidon. A woman from Canaan who was living there came to him pleading, 'Have mercy on me, O Lord, King David's Son! For my daughter has a demon within her, and it torments her constantly.' But Jesus gave her no reply—not even a word. Then his disciples urged him to send her away. 'Tell her to get going,' they said, 'for she is bothering us with all her begging.'" Matthew 15:21-23 (TLB)

The need of this woman's daughter brought her to Christ. Her request was short and to the point. Yet, He ignored her at first. How discouraging that must have been for her. His silence caused her to become even more insistent in obtaining mercy and favor from Him. Her persistence begging became annoying to those around her. Finally, out of frustration, the disciples asked Jesus to intervene. Although her persistence bothered the others, it most likely didn't bother Jesus. At another time He had said, "Ask and it will be given to you; seek and you will find; knock and the door will be opened to you" Matthew 7:7. Seeking and knocking requires persistence.

At last Jesus answered her, but His reply must have been disheartening to this mother seeking help for her daughter. He told her, "I was sent to help the Jews—the lost sheep of Israel—not the Gentiles" Matthew 15:24 (TLB). His response could have caused her to lose hope, become silent or even angry, if her confidence in Him to heal her daughter had not been strong.

Had He been testing this Canaanite woman's faith to prove it genuine? Had she originally come to Jesus with an arrogant attitude, demanding His assistance? Was His action attempting to make her realize this was not the way to approach Him? In her struggle, she came again, but more humbly and reverently, worshiping and kneeling before Him and pleaded again, "Sir, help me!" Then He replied, "It is not right to take the children's bread and toss it to the dogs" Matthew 15:26.

When we read Scripture, we read words. We don't hear the tone in which it was said or the look on the speaker's face. Was it said in anger, disgust, compassion or sorrow? Sometimes we can tell by the way a passage is written, but not always. We can also lose some of the original meaning, because the culture at that time was different from ours today.

At this time in history, the Jewish people looked with contempt upon the non-Jews, referring to them as dogs. However, in this Scripture, the original Greek word translated as *dog* means *puppy* or *little dogs*, which meant a pet dog in the home. When Jesus used the word *puppy*, it was not meant to refer to this woman in a derogatory way. Instead, He used it as an affectionate term. Even today we say, "Cute as a puppy." His answer was not meant to put her down or intimidate her, but to cause her to understand why He was not quick to assist her. He was pointing out to her that at that particular time He was sent to a certain group of people and she was not part of this group.

I think He answered her with compassion in His voice. Feeling His compassion, this woman felt confident to continue the conversation. She evidently understood that He was to go first to the Jews. In response, she continued the analogy: "Yes it is, Lord," she said. "Even the dogs eat the crumbs that fall from their master's table" Matthew 15:27.

Again, the original Greek word is *puppy*; even the puppies eat from their master's table. In other words, she was willing to wait her turn and take whatever was left over. This indicates to me that she was a very wise woman, as she quickly provided her defense. Jesus, knowing He had the ability to help her, saw her humility and strong faith. She came to Him pleading for mercy, recognizing Him as the Messiah, worshipping Him and simply pleading her case—Lord help me. He respected her for defending her cause. As a result, He granted her request: "Then Jesus said to her, "Woman, you have great faith! Your request is granted." And her daughter was healed at that moment" Matthew 15:28.

Since this woman came in faith, believing Jesus could heal her daughter, He did not reject her even though He tested her at first. His heart goes out to those who have complete confidence in Him. It is all about faith in the One who has the answers. He will always be with those who call out to Him. God is calling all His people into a closer walk with Him, so they will know Him as Abba Father, the One who cares.

Trust the Lord

> "Trust in the LORD with all your heart;
> do not depend on your own understanding.
> Seek his will in all you do,
> and he will show you which path to take."
> Proverbs 3:5-6 (NLT)

Troubling circumstances and feelings of helplessness could make life seem hopeless, at times. As we seek God's will in our lives, He will guide and direct us. He may also make the path we are on straighter, by removing obstacles, guiding us around them or through them, as we reach for our goal. Jesus said, "With man this is impossible, but with God all things are possible" Matthew 19:26. With His strength, you can endure and conquer the problems that come your way. When troubling times hit, you are not alone; God is always with you. David wrote:

> "Where can I go from your Spirit? Where can I flee from your presence? If I go up to the heavens, you are there; if I make my bed in the depths, you are there. If I rise on the wings of the dawn, if I settle on the far side of the sea, even there your hand will guide me, your right hand will hold me fast." Psalm 139:7-10

The Holy Spirit lives in you, and He will assist you as you travel through, around, over or under obstacles. Trouble is not supposed to overcome you. You are to overcome it. Encountering resistance builds strong character. The victory comes after a battle.

> Character cannot be developed in ease and quiet.
> Only through experiences of trials and suffering
> can the soul be strengthened, vision cleared,
> ambition inspired and success achieved.
> ~ Helen Keller

See challenges as the preparation for the victories of God. It is not what you are going through that is most important, but rather it is where you are going. What happens to good people when bad things happen to them? They become better people. Choose to be better rather than bitter. In her poem "Trouble is a Steppingstone to Growth," Helen Steiner Rice wrote, "For the grandeur of life is born of defeat. For in overcoming we make life complete."

Stay a Little While

My daughter stopped by unexpectedly to drop off a manual for me. I asked her if she was coming in. Her answer was no; she was running late for another errand. I would have liked her to stay a while. Do you take your prayers to God and just drop them off? Jesus said, "Look! I stand at the door and knock. If you hear me calling and open the door, I will come in, and we will share a meal as friends" Revelation 3:20 (NLT). Usually when meeting with a friend to have a meal together, we wouldn't be in a hurry to rush off right away. We would take the time to have a conversation and just enjoy each other's company. That is what God expects us to do when we come to meet with Him in prayer. He would like us to stay a while.

Deborah Oxendine's wrote about a vision God gave her in her book *Come Sup with Me*. She saw a table stretched out across heaven, "with no end in sight." A brilliant, sparkling white tablecloth covered it. Jesus took His place at the head of the table saying, "This is the table I told you I would prepare for you in the presence of your enemies." She was told a royal banquet was on the table, but all she could see was the brilliant white tablecloth. Jesus said, "It can only be seen with the eyes of your spirit....It's all here, everything you could ever want or need, healing, deliverance, grace, finances, strength... everything is waiting for you....All you have to do is sit down and partake of it."

He went on to explain to her that people come in and out to drop off their prayers and praises, but they don't bother to stay. If they would stay awhile, they could take their needs and their requests right off the table. They wouldn't have to wait for an answer, because they could take what they needed with them.

Is the Lord asking you to stay a while or are you too busy? Prayer is important, because God has the answers to your questions. He is the One who will meet all your needs and the One who will surround you with all His love. You are free to dine with Him. Your chair is waiting for you. He invites you to come.

PART 3

Peace Found at Last

God's specialty is the impossible

Chapter 9

Opportunities

We all go through tough times now and then, but perspective makes a difference. When tough times arrive, approach them with the hope that things will get better. Be on the lookout for lessons or opportunities that present themselves. For example, some problems teach self-control and patience, as in traffic congestion. Did you know the first traffic jam was in 1879? In New York City the carriages, horses and handcarts brought the Broadway to a halt for five hours.

Recently, an article in our local newspaper related the tragic event of a synagogue fire that destroyed the sanctuary, along with hundreds of prayer books and sacred ritual items. The building was left unusable, but even from loss blessings can flow. The blessings of compassion and commitment from the community and churches led the Rabbi Ron Muroff to state, "A new life chapter begins following loss—but only if we choose it."

Even in the worst situations, God is able to show you the possibilities, the way out or new opportunities. The rest is up to you. Missed opportunities might show up later in a similar situation. This is an opportunity to practice what you learned and react differently. Every day becomes a new beginning.

No matter what happens, as hard as it seems at the time, never give up. Goals and dreams may change through the years, but you always have the values that are important to you. If you are not sure what your values are or would like to define them in more detail, the article "What Are Your Values?" on www.mindtools.com is very helpful. You will find life can be much easier when you acknowledge your values and make plans and decisions that honor them.

Having confidence in Jesus and in all He did for you causes God's mercy and grace to flow your way. The best news is: your sins aren't held against you anymore; they are forgiven. Sin's control over you was destroyed. Any defilement and shame was cleansed. You received eternal life as an ongoing gift, along with His favor and blessings.

The right to tap into the Lord's strength and power is now yours. The Holy Spirit, who came to reside in you, will direct and guide you. Wisdom and knowledge, you wouldn't normally have, becomes available through the Holy Spirit. Your name changed too. It is no longer "sinner," but "forgiven; a child of God." Because of the sacrifice of Jesus, many people are accepted as righteous before a holy God, resulting in the adoption of multitudes as His children and heirs. I heard the Lord say:

> "Sin or shame is not a stumbling block for me. I have created the antidote and given it to the world. As some seek wellness and others find comfort in their misery, some will seek the antidote I offer and find the wellness that leads to eternal life, and others will

continue to find comfort in their sins. I am here, waiting for my people to come to me. Come and be surrounded by my love."

Balls Bounce Back

Over the years, it was hard not to notice that problems came at me in various degrees and in various ways. Looking back over my life, it seems to have been a roller coaster of one distressing season after another. Sometimes I felt that I hardly had a chance to catch my breath in-between. Abuse, divorce, depression, cancer and family lies have all stopped to visit. I asked God more than once, "Why does life have to be so hard?"

I think I can safely say that we all had a problem or two come our way that we wished traveled on by. Whatever trouble or hardships come into our lives, with God we can make it through and come out the other side better people. To be defeated should not be an option.

For many years, I gathered colorful bouncing balls in a glass fishbowl that has become quite a collection. It is comprised of balls in all colors and styles. I often wondered why I like balls enough to collect them. Then one day I felt God telling me that my ball collection was to be a reminder to me—a rubber ball, despite its color, style or size will always bounce back and I can too.

- ❖ My "happy smile" ball reminds me of the Scripture that says, "A happy heart makes the face cheerful" Proverbs 15:13.

- ❖ The different sized balls remind me that problems come in different sizes—some big, some small. Even more important, blessings come in different sizes too.
- ❖ The one that looks like the earth reminds me that God is our creator.

The Lord used my ball collection to make sure I knew that no matter what I went through, with Him on my side, I could always bounce back and you can too!

The Pruning

"Within the last several years we have endured many such prunings," an overwhelmed husband wrote. His wife and his son had suffered many serious issues, including numerous surgeries and life-changing diseases. "I become weary from the snips of the pruning shears in my life," he added. He was referring to the following Scripture: "I am the true vine, and my Father is the gardener. He cuts off every branch in me that bears no fruit, while every branch that does bear fruit he prunes so that it will be even more fruitful" John 15:1-2.

This writer thought God caused their bouts of sickness to prune them. He thought since God is all knowing, then He knew what was good for them—a referral to bringing pain and sickness into their lives for their good. I would beg to differ with this perception.

It is true that God corrects His children as any loving parent would. See Ephesians 6:4. However, the Bible warns parents not to exasperate or provoke their children. Colossians 3:21 (NLB) tells fathers, "Don't scold your children so much that they become discouraged and quit trying." The Bible instructs us to bring our children up in the training and instruction of the Lord. How did Jesus train and instruct His disciples? He taught God's way of living and corrected by setting the example of living the life He taught. Sometimes He used stories, parables or strong words to help get His point across. Yet, He was always the epitome of love for others and represented the love of His heavenly Father.

Some people point to the Old Testament, also known as the Old Covenant. Here many events indicate God brought suffering or punishment on His people to teach them obedience to His commandments. The truth is that after the death of Jesus Christ, Christians moved into a different dispensation and a different relationship with God. We are now living under a New Covenant, as described in the New Testament.

This doesn't mean God won't allow life to take its natural course. God's Word instructs us how to live. Our parents instruct us how to live. Only quite often, we find out things for ourselves or should I say, "learn lessons" as we walk through this journey of life. Yet in the midst of trouble, we find Him stepping in and turning those negative events around to bring positive results, increasing our confidence in His goodness and kindness. What is meant for evil, He flips around and uses to produce something good. He promises that all that happens to you, He will work together for something beneficial, if you love Him and are fitting into His plans.

The dictionary says "prune" means to remove unnecessary parts, to remove anything considered superfluous or undesirable. Superfluous means excessive, unnecessary or needless. The word for prune in the original Greek text meant to prune, clear unproductive wood, or *cleanse*. Jesus's own blood, which He willingly sacrificed for us, *cleansed* us from sin and shame. After accepting Jesus Christ as our Savior,

God begins pruning off condemnation and the tendency to sin—the unnecessary, unproductive areas of our lives. This takes place with the leading and nudging of the Holy Spirit in a person's life. God's deep love draws us into obedience to His way.

Let's be careful not to blame Him for the undesirable and destructive events that come into our lives. He is not the cause or source of pain and hardship in the lives of the ones He calls His children. He is the source of their help.

Who's at Fault?

I have witnessed people who use God as a scapegoat, instead of looking to Him for hope, help and comfort. Every time something goes wrong or when something bad happens, they want to blame Him. Certainly many situations are tragic and painful, and loss can feel unbearable, but don't be quick to blame Him for things that go wrong in life.

I once heard a reporter ask this question concerning an accident victim, "Why do you think God took his life?" I was shocked that he would even think to ask such a question of the suffering person left behind. The truth is the victim lost his life because of a decision another person made. That other person decided to drive his car despite the fact he had over the safe limit of alcohol flowing through his bloodstream, hampering his thought processes and responses. God was in no way responsible for taking that person's life.

When dealing with problems, be careful not to turn away from God or act as if they were His fault. Be careful not to fall into the trap of permitting troubles that come your way to separate you from Him. Run to Him, not from Him. He is your support during stressful times:

Opportunities

> "I will sing of your strength,
> in the morning I will sing of your love;
> for you are my fortress,
> my refuge in times of trouble."
> Psalm 59:16

After I heard of the terrible plane crash that took the life of Dr. Myles Munroe, his wife and several other leaders from his church, I felt crushed. How could this happen to this loyal man of God and the others with him? Then shortly after this, John Paul Jackson lost his life to an illness. They are needed here I lamented. "How and Why?" seems to be our first questions during such times. Why didn't God intervene and stop it from happening? My husband reminded me that people in heaven aren't standing in line to come back here. But my question still was, "Why didn't He intervene?" My husband's wise and inspired answer was, "Because He decided to give them their reward now."

Even though we wish our loved ones or those we cared about were still here, they are happy and grateful to be in heaven amidst the love of Jesus and their heavenly Father. Yet I wanted to hear directly from the Lord about this. I prayed, "Lord, you know I pray your will be done. But it hurts when I see men that you have used so mightily leave us. They still seem so young to me with so much more to accomplish." I heard the Lord reply, "These men walked with me; they deserve their reward. Others are in place to rise up and fill the vacuum that they left behind. Your time will come too. Death separates you from time and allows you to walk into eternity; a spectacular life compared to life here."

I want my readers to know—God does not plan all tragedy or cause it. At times, the choices we make affect us in a negative way. The decisions of others can affect us in a positive or negative way. It could also be possible that the evil one's influence is working undercover in certain situations. The book of Ecclesiastes adds that time and chance happen to us all.

I asked the Lord how He felt about all this. He answered:

> "This is an answer for you to understand. I look down upon the earth and see calamity and heartache. I see my little ones in dire straits. My focus is on my Son's return, that all may know my love, that all may know my ways. See and know my ways. This earth and those in it bring enough evil and heartache on themselves. I stand and watch and shake my head at the antics of my creation. When will they seek me and know my ways?
>
> Sin has consequences. Goodness has rewards. And remember that time and chance do happen, as my son Solomon wrote. I have set in place principles and laws. Living within those bounds or out of those bounds cause natural reactions, some for good and some for bad. That is why it is important to learn my ways and apply them in your life.
>
> In times past, I kept a heavy hand upon the nations, especially upon my people. They were to be an example of my blessings to the rest of the world. But they were more interested in serving themselves, then in serving

me. Today there is a new dispensation. I call out the ones that will serve me and love me. They are a nation among all nations. An example of my love and my goodness among the darkness and evil that prevails.

When my Son brings the fullness of my kingdom upon the earth, He will also come prepared for war. Then the nations will receive their just due. Now is a time of waiting and preparation for this time to come."

Hope

A turn of a radio knob, a push of a television button or a glance at the paper and the news highlights for us the violence, the abuse and the tragedies taking place in our world today. Hurting, broken hearts are everywhere. Pills abound for depression, tension, anxiety and stress. Is there no hope, no one to turn to, no one to understand, no one to help? Some people meet times that seem as if all is lost and things could not be worse. Maybe you have been there. Maybe you are in that spot right now. All you can see is trouble. You go through the motions of living, but are so drained emotionally and physically you feel as though you are barely holding on. With so much trouble, you feel like you can hardly keep your head above water.

Suicide is the only relief some can find. If you have thought about this consider: although you can see only your own pain at this moment, the pain you will leave behind in the hearts of those who love you and care for you will be unending and will follow them for a lifetime. If you think no one cares, then you believe the lie of the enemy. Pastor Willy Rice of Calvary Church in Clearwater, Florida said, "It is a tragic solution, because it is a final answer to a *temporary* situation." I want you to know that the hurt you feel today will not always be there. So do not give up.

We have the example of Job in the Bible who came to such a place in his own life. He had led a life blessed in every way. Without warning, his sons and daughters were killed and his prosperity destroyed. Finally his health left him, as he sat in ashes with his body covered in terribly painful boils. He was full of despair and hopelessness. He questioned God's sense of justice. He felt He did nothing to deserve this. Job wondered where God was when he needed His help. He wanted to know when his pain was going to end. He came to the point that he decided he wanted to die. He just wanted to stop hurting.

Our enemy known as Satan instigated the pain and horror that came suddenly upon Job. God didn't, but He did allow it. He also limited what Satan could bring against Job—he was not permitted to take his life. It all started with a talk between God and Satan. God was proud of Job's righteousness and love for Him. Satan said it was just because God blessed him. He continued telling God that if He would take away Job's blessings then he would turn against Him. God wanted to prove to Satan that this was not true. And God was right. Even Job's wife told him to curse God and die, but he refused to turn against God. To reward Job for his continued faithfulness, He blessed him twice as much in the end.

We see only a piece of the big picture, but God sees it all, the beginning and the end. Pastor Willy Rice used a very helpful analogy. He likened it to a jigsaw puzzle. Once all the pieces are dumped out of the box, you see a mess, a jumble of all sorts of pieces. Picking up one piece, it may look dark and like a blob. As soon as that one dark piece is put in place with the rest of the pieces, it turns into a completed picture that is beautiful. He summed this analogy up by saying, "Even when your little piece doesn't make any sense, put your trust in the living God, who knows how all the pieces go together. His presence and power is what we need."

There once was a man who never gave up on his goal and vision for his future, no matter how hard life became. This man came from humble beginnings, being born on the road as his parents traveled out of town. While he was still a young child, it was rumored that he would be a future king. The present king, not willing to give up his throne to anyone, sought the death of this young boy. Hearing about the king's plans, the boy's parents fled for safety from their family home to another country. They returned to their original home only after the death of this wicked king. Later this growing boy lost his father and helped his mother continue to raise his many brothers and sisters.

He worked for a while in his father's construction business, but eventually he started a thriving ministry. As his ministry was getting under way, he was informed his cousin had been murdered. Within a short time, some people became jealous of his growing ministry and tried to cause problems for him. Then his chosen treasurer and friend betrayed him to earn additional money for himself. To add insult to injury, this young man was arrested on false charges, while a faithful friend and active worker in his ministry denied even knowing him. On top of all this, hired liars testified against him during an illegal trial. As a result, a large group of people believed the rumors of those perpetual liars and called for his death.

This young man did not deserve the suffering that became a part of his life. He had been a loving, caring and selfless servant to the people during his short adult life. Through it all, his love and dedication to his purpose and goal never wavered. In the end, he willingly gave his life for the greater good of humanity. His name was Jesus, the awaited Christ, God's Son, the Messiah sent by God to free humanity from the penalty of their sin and shame. The Bible explains the result of the things Jesus suffered:

> "Even though Jesus was God's Son, he learned obedience from the things he suffered. In this way, God qualified him as a perfect High Priest, and he became the source of eternal salvation for all those who obey him." Hebrews 5:8-9 (NLT)

Jesus was oppressed, afflicted, imprisoned and falsely tried. Without saying a word in His defense, they led Him away to His death. Yet who realized in His day, He willingly suffered the punishment for their sins. Isaiah prophesied: "He was despised and rejected—a man of sorrows, acquainted with deepest grief. We turned our backs on him and looked the other way. He was despised, and we did not care" Isaiah 53:3 (NLT). Isaiah 53:4-9 tells us that Jesus carried our sorrows, our troubles, our pain, our sickness and the guilt of our sins.

The life story of the One who never sinned continues. After He gave Himself to be an offering for our sins, died and was even buried, He was resurrected. In other words, God brought Him back to life, assuring us of the possibility of eternal life with a loving God. Jesus spent another forty days on this earth with more than 500 witnesses. Despite everything Jesus had to suffer and the anguish He endured, He found satisfaction in what His sacrifice accomplished. He died to forgive our past and rose to restore our future.

Jesus is our hope. We can turn to Him. He knows what it is like to suffer. This enables Him to understand and help us. In Romans 8:34, we read, "Christ Jesus who died—more than that, who was raised to life—is at the right hand of God and is also interceding for us."

Be assured, He will come to your rescue. He has not forgotten you, so do not lose hope. Continue to trust Him. Troubles and heartaches are temporary, a speck in time when compared to eternity.

Chapter 10

Comforting Prayer

I once heard a person pronounce from the pulpit that he didn't understand why we should pray, especially if an immediate response from God wasn't received. This concerned me. He also said he didn't know why he should pray, when he had to wait for those who committed offenses and injustices against him to receive their judgment. He added that he felt he had a relationship with God for many years, but still didn't see why we should pray. That was scary to me since he was speaking from the pulpit. It made me wonder how many regular folk may have this same question.

Many people know it is possible to have a relationship with God, because they have experienced it. I hope you experience this relationship, this closeness with the Lord too. Studying the Bible or having a position in the church does not necessarily mean a relationship with God is established. For example, I saw this person and heard him speak. I was told his name. I knew what he looked like. I could say I know who he is, but do I have a relationship with him? No. He knows nothing about me and even if he were told about me, we still would not have a relationship. Why? Because we never spent time together. We have not corresponded.

We have not talked. We don't know each other on a personal level.

Relationships are developed by talking with each other and getting to know what the other person is all about. This also requires spending time together. A relationship with God is established in the same way—by talking with Him and spending time with Him. And you do that through prayer. A person becomes familiar with who He is by reading about Him or hearing about Him, but a relationship doesn't exist unless time is spent together. There is no way to begin to describe how fulfilling and satisfying it is to have a relationship with our Lord; the desire to keep searching for something more no longer exists. You have found all there is.

I have also heard of people who discourage others from having this relationship with the Lord. These people evidently decided, since it was not true for them, the possibility of such a relationship must be a false teaching. But I will tell you, when I talk with my heavenly Father about my happy times, my sad times, my past, my future, my family, my friends and life in general, it never occurred to me that I didn't have a relationship with Him. The words *father*, *friend* and *children* all indicate a relationship. These are terms God uses repeatedly throughout Scripture to describe His bond with us.

This relationship is one of the things that separates Christianity from other religions. We do not have a god made by the hands of man or some far away god. He is neither unloving nor uninvolved. We have a living God who loves us and wants to be involved in our lives. He desires it. It's possible. Millions of Christians enjoy this closeness. It is natural when you love someone, to want to be close to each other. It is the same with God. "You will seek me and find me when you seek me with all your heart" Jeremiah 29:13. "Come near to God and he will come near to you" James 4:8.

When people desire to be close to Him and want to know Him better, they begin to understand what knowing Him and having a relationship with Him is all about. As time is spent together, a relationship with Him is born without even thinking about it. Job's experience led him to say, "My ears had heard of you, but now my eyes have seen you" Job 42:5.

Stay close to Him by going into the sanctuary, into the Holy of Holies, to meet with Him. While there, listen in your heart for Him. Often He speaks in whispers. Listen closely. He is in the habit of speaking to His people, but you need to listen in order to hear Him. Jesus said His people would know His voice. A word of caution: the Bible also warns of false teachers and other false voices. Whatever you feel the Lord is saying or impressing on your heart will always line up with Scripture and His character.

Many people think of prayer as asking God for things or asking for His intervention, but prayer is much more than this. It is revealing your heart to Him and having Him reveal His heart to you. Every day He waits for you to come and enjoy rest in His presence.

Here and There

Instead of spending time with Him, do you keep running here and running there? Be careful your busyness and excuses do not drip over into your relationship with the very God who gives life and loves you with all His heart. Search your heart. Has He been missing you? Go to Him and stay a little while. Dance for Him. Follow Him. Avoid running to the right and to the left. Stop running here and there, but run to Him. He resides in the Holy of Holies, where he waits for you to come and visit Him. So take a break from your busyness and your burdens, and fellowship with the Lord. Leave behind the cares of this world and walk with Him.

Join Him and He will open the doors for you to walk through. When you call to Him, He will answer. In a psalm of thanks to the Lord, David wrote, "Splendor and majesty are before him; strength and joy are in his dwelling place....Give thanks to the Lord, for he is good; his love endures forever" 1 Chronicles 16:27, 34. He is waiting for you, always waiting for you. Sit with Him and enjoy His company. Take His hand and He will lead you.

When I go to the Lord with questions, with situations I need help in or with requests for others, I know I will receive an answer. Sometimes I go to God and tell Him I am feeling lonely and I feel His love surround me. I go to Him with my tears and feel His comfort. I go to Him feeling weak and come away feeling strong. I go to Him feeling confused and come away with direction. I go to Him with praise and thankfulness for all He is and for everything He has done. This is relationship. It results in a knowing, an understanding, an interaction and a feeling of closeness.

Have you ever thought about praying without asking for a thing? Have you ever gone to Him in prayer, because you want to be in His presence just because you love Him or because you want to feel close to Him? In a dream I heard the Lord say:

> "Some come to me because they need me. They feel desperate. They don't know who else to turn to. When no one else will meet their needs, they turn to me. This is *The Kiss of Need*.

Some people never kiss me. They never come to me. They feel they have no need of me. They do not love me. I am of no significance in their lives. This is *No Kisses*.

There are those that come to me just because they love me. They enjoy being in my presence. Oh, they know I can meet their needs, but that is not the only time they come to me. These people want to be close to me all the time. This is *The Kiss of Love*."

My question to you is this: "What kind of kisses do you give?"

Rejoice

"Rejoice in the Lord always. I will say it again: Rejoice!" Philippians 4:4

Re-joice means joy again and again. Joy isn't dependent on what is happening around you at the moment. Joy differs from happiness, because it does not depend on circumstances. It comes from realizing God will always be there for you, helping you though whatever obstacles come your way. Paul wrote, "Rejoice always, pray continually, give thanks in all circumstances; for this is God's will for you in Christ Jesus" 1 Thessalonians 5:16-18.

"If God is for us, who can be against us?" Romans 8:3. God's name, "I AM," expresses His characteristics of dependability, faithfulness and of eternal stability. He expects the full trust of His people. He is God of the past, present and future. He cares what happens in your life. While David was in the Desert of Judah, he wrote:

> "I lie awake at night thinking of you—of how much you have helped me—and how I rejoice through the night beneath the protecting shadow of your wings. I follow close behind you, protected by your strong right arm." Psalm 63:6-8 (TLB)

Even though Jesus was teaching His disciples to believe in Him, He occasionally asked them why they doubted. How often do we find ourselves doubting, when He is the One who can help us? What is impossible for us becomes God's opportunity.

After Jesus rose from the grave, He went to His disciples. They had gathered in a locked room, except for Thomas, in fear of the Jews who had demanded Jesus's death. Jesus appeared in the room showing them the scars on His hands and side where the nails and spear had entered during His crucifixion. When Thomas heard that Jesus had appeared to them, he refused to believe it. He doubted; he wanted proof. A week later, Thomas was with the disciples when they had gathered in the house again. Jesus was willing to walk through locked doors to meet with him and the other disciples. He told Thomas to put his finger in His hands where the nails had been placed and his hand into His side. He gave him the proof, the reason to believe. Jesus then said to him, "Stop doubting and believe." Jesus invited Thomas to believe and He gives us the same invitation.

> *What is impossible for us becomes God's opportunity.*

The people who don't know Jesus suffer alone, but you have a God who will never leave you—not even during the bad times or in your moments of greatest despair. You can depend on Him and trust Him to be with you. You can rely on the Holy Spirit to comfort you. You can know God has the answers you are looking for.

- Rejoice because God is with you.
- Rejoice because God will see you through.
- Rejoice because Jesus intercedes for you.
- Rejoice because your sins are forgiven.
- Rejoice because eternity with God lies ahead.

Enjoy and savor His graciousness and His mercy. It was for love that He sent His son to this world and it is for love that He stands by you in the good times and in the bad times. He is waiting for you to know Him, believe Him and trust Him. Then you can sing for joy because all is well in Him. Nehemiah tells us, "for the joy of the Lord is your strength" Nehemiah 8:10. It is His desire for you, His loved one, to be strengthened and filled with His joy and His peace. I heard the Lord say:

> "Tell my people, it is time. It is time for them to come to me, to seek me. Come to me. Come everyone. Let me hold you. Let me help you. Let me heal your wounds. I will come in great power to restore and bring restoration. There is joy in my heart. Let me impart my joy to you. There is peace in my presence. Come, sense my peace. Love encircles me. Be

consumed by my love for you. Rejoice in this day. Yet again, I say rejoice."

When we truly appreciate the Lord and all He has and wants for us, it becomes so easy to sing to Him with thanksgiving. Again, I heard the Lord:

"Call upon me and I will answer. Rise up and worship me. For I am your God, even the God of this whole earth. For I have created it and it waits for me. Yes, even my return. Praise me. How I love your praises. How I love the praises of my people. They are soothing to my soul. Yes, rejoice in me. For surely the time will come when my joy shall cover the earth."

His Comfort

The Lord is calling you to Himself. It's time to rejoice because there is peace in His presence and a joy that overflows. Let Him comfort you with His Word. He has come that you may have peace. Find the peace and tranquility that you desire through Him. Let Him fill your empty spaces with His love, letting it surround and overtake you. Sometimes you need to step back and watch what He will do. All power is in His hands. There is nothing impossible for Him. Healing abounds in His presence.

It is said there is a way that seems right to a man but it leads only to death. True life is in Jesus. Following after Him leads to blessings and joy to fill your soul. His love for you lasts forever.

He knows where you have come from, where you have been and now He wants to guide you into your future. Go to Him now that He may care for you, bless you and heal you. Find rest in His strong comforting arms. Life is in His hands, so don't stray. Stay close. Walk hand in hand with your God and all will be well. The Lord calls to you saying:

> "Come, come away with Me. Let Me fill your heart and soul with my peace. I liken my way to the streams of living water that run without end and bring blessings wherever it flows. So follow in my way and blessings will flow to all you touch."

Chapter 11

New Memories

> "You will keep in perfect peace those whose minds are steadfast, because they trust in you. Trust in the LORD forever, for the LORD, the LORD himself, is the Rock eternal."
> Isaiah 26:3-4

Trusting in God means you believe Him. Trusting God means you know He can help you with the situations that come your way. It means if you don't have the answer or solution, you know that He does. You trust Him completely, not just now and then, but always. Sharing your problems with God doesn't mean blocking them out of your mind. Problems will try to manage you, but acknowledging and managing them will put you in charge.

When someone treats you badly, it is terribly hurtful. Unfortunately, you cannot change others. Pastor Joel Hunter at Northland Church in Longwood, Florida said, "You can't change or fix anyone else. That should take the weight of the world off your shoulders. You can't even fix you. You have to look to Jesus."

Sometimes the irritations and frustrations that come from everyday interactions with others can get to us. It doesn't have to be some big thing. It helps to remember we are each uniquely made, a product of God's creativity. And we are each on our own journey through this life. Our experiences and upbringings can be very different, so it shouldn't be a surprise that our responses are also very different.

The Holy Spirit helps us live lives that please God and that may mean changing our reactions to others around us. Peace keeps its distance as long as we project our "shoulds" and "oughts" on others. Feelings won't change until our beliefs change, until our perception of an event changes. In Romans 12:2, we read, "Do not conform to the pattern of this world, but be transformed by the renewing of your mind." This transformation takes time and is ongoing. Christ becomes the center of our lives—no matter what happens around us. God's purpose and plan for us is to become like His Son, to be conformed to His likeness.

Setting aside frustrations and irritations is not always easy to do. But rather than being overly concerned or worrying about what others are doing, think about how to be a light and make a difference. It can help us when we focus on their needs and are of service to them. As God fills us with His love and compassionate, it's time to move into helping and encouraging others.

When hurtful memories want to come back relentlessly to bother you, give yourself something else to fill some of the space those continual thoughts take. See how much good is in your life instead of focusing on what needs to be fixed or what is wrong. Be more conscious of the answer and the One who brings the answer. Always keep in mind, hard times will pass away. They are not here to stay. Try these simple alternatives:

- Remember the good things, the good times.
- Thank God for your blessings.
- Spend time in God's presence and Word.
- Minister to others.

Rehashing the Past

A tragic or traumatic incident that comes our way can become all-consuming. Letting go of a painful, hurtful occurrence is difficult for many of us. I asked myself, "Why is it so hard to stop reliving a bad experience?" as each recalled memory blazed a deeper crevice in my mind. I decided it was because I didn't want to accept what happened. I didn't want it to be part of my life. I didn't want it to happen.

Continually rehashing the past or bringing up the wrongdoings of others will not provide relief. Many times, past events are rehashed because we think we didn't take the right action at the time. We are still trying to "fix it," even if it is only in our own minds. Gary Chapman wrote, "I am amazed by how many individuals mess up every new day with yesterday. They insist on bringing into today the failures of yesterday and in so doing, they pollute a potentially wonderful day."[1]

Unfortunately, we can't go back and change the past. It is OK to accept the hurt and pain that went along with the negative event that happened. Acceptance allows you to move forward again. Once you stop trying to change the past, a sense of closure takes place. Then go on to the good news; you can make a new tomorrow. That you can do.

Upsetting Thoughts

When you think about it, how true or helpful are your negative thoughts? Do the things you say and think make it hard for you to work and enjoy your life? Pessimistic, unhelpful thoughts can increase your worry or fear and lead to anxiety or depression. They can affect how you feel and keep you from sleeping well.

Studies show that when you change what you think, you can change your mood. Paul wrote, "We take captive every thought to make it obedient to Christ" 2 Corinthians 10:5. Once we become aware of our unwanted thoughts, we are able to call them out. For example, if you are worried you might lose your job, tell yourself, "I am having the *thought* I might lose my job." This is a reminder to yourself that it is a thought and not reality.

I've become more aware of my own thoughts as I've been writing this book. I am amazed at how easily and how regularly the thoughts about unfavorable events pop-up in my mind, compared to the enjoyable times that I would rather remember. If thoughts about a disturbing situation distract me, I remind myself that I have discussed it with the Lord and He is taking care of it. Other times I'll start singing. Singing or praising God stops unwanted thoughts in their tracks.

With time and practice, we can actually identify which of our thoughts affect problems or cause upset feelings. Then we can go on to replace these unsettling thoughts with more accurate and helpful statements that encourage, instead of entertaining negative thoughts that discourage. An article by Krissy Brady relates this interesting research:

"When we think about emotionally charged events, we end up dwelling on how embarrassed or hurt we felt and perpetually relive the same awful feelings over and over again. Focusing on the negative experiences increases our unwanted emotions, which makes us see more negative things until they're all we see," says clinical psychologist Elizabeth Lombardo, Ph.D. "It's like pushing on a bruise. It doesn't feel good and it prevents healing."

New research suggests that focusing on the *context* of a crappy memory—like what you ate that day or what you wore—instead of thinking about how you *felt*, aids in alleviating the stress spiral these memories create.

In an April 2014 study led by Florin Dolcos, Ph.D., a psychology professor at the University of Illinois, participants had to recall their most emotional negative memories while their brains were being scanned by MRI....After comparing the brain scans, the researchers found that when participants thought about the non-emotional aspects of the memory, activity in their brains' emotional centers decreased, and they reported fewer icky feelings.

This method of focusing on context...allows you to acknowledge the memory while decreasing the level of stress connected to it."[2]

Another thing you may find helpful is to write down unconstructive, harassing thoughts about negative events, and then rip them up and throw them away. Think of it as tossing away your gloomy thoughts. It signals your brain that you are getting past the bad stuff. If you hold on to the paper, your brain will think you want to keep those thoughts too, causing them to replay. As much as the past wants to control today or your future, don't let it. It is to your benefit to stop giving it authority over your life. Determine it is over and start a new life, one that doesn't permit past hurtful events to influence today or your tomorrows.

Decide life will flow from your thoughts and your emotions. Embracing all the negative things brings the opposite of what you really want in your life. Instead, embrace God. You are important to Him and your life counts. His love and grace send blessings your way. He wants every good thing for you. He is not like others; He will always love you and He will always be there for you. Grin, smile and be happy because He is with you. Do you hear the Lord speaking to your heart? He is saying:

> "Come to me and see that I am good. Hold on to me tight. I'll never let you go. You are mine and I am yours. Don't fret. Don't fret about tomorrow. I have all your cares in my hands.
>
> Bring to me your worship, your love and your dance. It pleases me so. Here pain is erased. It is not eternal, but only for a season. Look forward to the life you have in me. Dance for joy. Rejoice. Arise out of the depths of sadness. Let the light shine. Happiness is in the air."

Another Perspective

How should we react to offenses, hurt and injustices? In one way or another, we have to deal with the feelings they cause. I heard a speaker relate many personal stories from his life. They reflected what he saw or felt when he or someone he knew was being hurt, taken advantage of or treated in a demeaning way. I kept waiting for the encouraging, happy endings, but they never came. His stories had no closure. His summary, as I understood it, was this: although he wanted immediate justice, he had to be satisfied in knowing justice would come with the return of Christ on the great Judgment Day, a time when God returns to the earth and intervenes with judgment or rewards.

To those of you who may feel the same way, I would like to give you another alternative to the ending of his stories and to your stories. Rather than waiting for God's revenge or His final judgment, which will come because He won't put up with sin forever—may I suggest forgiving those who have offended you and asking God to intervene in that person's life. Jesus did tell us to pray for our enemies. You could pray that He reveal Himself to the offender, bringing change in that person through His love.

Consider that at times, positive results are found in hurtful or offensive experiences. For example, as weights cause the resistance to build stronger muscles, unpleasant experiences cause the resistance to help build our spiritual muscles, our spiritual character. Here are some positive results produced from bad situations:

- They often give us the chance to practice patience.
- Praying for our enemies becomes a new habit.
- The opportunity arises to let the love God shows us spill over to others.
- Compassion for those experiencing similar situations is built.
- You may even see in yourself a response you would like to change.

The need to forgive also becomes apparent. Just as God showed us mercy, now we have the opportunity to show mercy to others. Mercy is being compassionate and kind toward an offender, refraining from the enforcement of a right and exhibiting patience and self-control.

Medad Birungi wrote, "Allowing yourself to hang on to hard feelings and become bitter only causes your wound to become even more infected spiritually. Honestly ask yourself, what good is it doing you to hold on to the hurt and bitterness that the Enemy has tried to plant within you?"[3]

Our response to such situations reveals how well we are doing or reveals areas that may still need work. In all we do, let's strive to be representatives of God's way. Peter put it this way:

> "So be truly glad. There is wonderful joy ahead, even though you have to endure many trials for a little while. These trials will show that your faith is genuine. It is being tested as fire tests and purifies gold—though your faith is far more precious than mere gold. So when your faith remains strong through many trials, it will bring you much praise and glory and honor on the day when Jesus Christ is revealed to the whole world." 1 Peter 1:6-7 (NLT)

The way to deal with hurt is to practice mercy and add to it grace, which is showing goodwill, kindness and favor. Willingly lay down everything that has hurt you. Forgiveness can accomplish this. Forgiving others releases the need to keep bringing up an offense, rehashing it and anguishing over it. The hurtful memories won't keep coming back to haunt you at the pace they once did. The anguish and pain those memories once brought with them will begin to diminish or dissolve. You cannot have mercy for yourself and justice for others, so choose to forgive and walk in freedom.

It is all right to move out from the suffering of past events and get on with a brighter future. Instead of dwelling on what was, begin to reach for what is ahead. Then you can say with Paul, "But one thing I do: forgetting what is behind and straining toward what is ahead" Philippians 3:13.

God Knows You

God looks both ways in your life and cups you in His hands. He knows your past and He sees your future. He is with you now. He is not restricted by time since He is the One who created it:

> "And God said, "Let there be light," and there was light. God saw that the light was good, and he separated the light from the darkness. God called the light "day," and the darkness he called "night." And there was evening, and there was morning—the first day." Genesis 1:3-5

The Lord can bring healing to your past hurts when you realize His presence was always there. He can look back to see when you were hurt, or when you began to accept things about yourself or about Him that were not true. Ask Him to speak to you about those wounded areas in your life to bring truth and healing. You were never alone and you never will be.

It was not God's original plan for bad things to happen. He did not intend for abuse to take place, or accidents to happen or for sickness to occur. He created a beautiful earth for us to populate and take care of. It is written, "God saw all that he had made, and it was very good" Genesis 1:31.

A point often overlooked is that He gives us a choice: choose life or choose death—His way or our way. That same choice was given to the first man and woman, Adam and Eve. God placed two trees in the garden where they lived. The Tree of Life represented His way of perfect love and eternal life. The Tree of Good and Evil represented man's way of compromise and choosing for himself what was right or wrong. This choice would lead to both a spiritual and physical death.

God warned Adam not to eat the fruit from the Tree of Good and Evil. But doubt in God's goodness and character, instigated by the devil, caused curiosity to overtake Adam and Eve. They choose the tree that would change and damage the future of humanity from its original intended design forever, that is, until Jesus stepped in.

We could ask God why He allowed the devil, disguised as a serpent, into the Garden of Eden. Why did He allow Adam and Eve to listen to the serpent's deceiving lies? In addition, why didn't He stop them from disobeying, since their decisions would lead humanity on a downward spiral? The answers to these questions lie in the fact that God created us with the ability to make our own decisions. Although He never approves of sin, abuse or wrongdoing of any kind, He allows every person to make his own choices whether for good or for evil. I heard the Lord say:

> "My love is deep and escapes no one. But all don't desire me or my love. They may choose. Their lives are the consequences of their

choices. Many choose me and let me reign in their lives. I will gently nudge, guide, and direct them on life's journey, but they may still choose to accept my way or rebel against me. My desire is that all may come to me with a deep desire to know me, to accept me as the God who loves them and cares for them."

As much as you would like to change areas in your past that were hurtful, those times are now part of your history. Unfortunately, past wounds can continue to fester affecting you today. God loves you and wants to bring truth and healing to the wounded areas in your heart. Hold those areas up to Him, letting Him shine His light on them. As His presence soaks those memories, healing begins to take place.

Chapter 12

Blessing of Peace

"The Lord gives strength to his people;
the Lord blesses his people with peace." Psalm 29:11

Is inner peace missing in your life? Do you feel troubled, on edge, unhappy or bothered? Do you long for peace? Do you search for harmony, satisfaction, serenity, calm and quietness for your soul? Then it is time to receive His blessing:

"The Lord bless you
and keep you;
the Lord make his face shine on you
and be gracious to you;
the Lord turn his face toward you
and give you peace."
Numbers 6:24-26

My journey to embrace this inner peace has been the longest and hardest for me. So many situations in life can cause feelings of being agitated, unsettled or resentful. Fears and worries kept me on edge. Job's situation finally caused him to say, "I have no peace, no quietness; I have no rest, but only turmoil" Job 3:26.

Together we will go through a few key issues, and from there I hope you will continue your journey with your own reflections, study and talks with the Lord. Jesus said, "Peace I leave with you; my peace I give you. I do not give to you as the world gives. Do not let your hearts be troubled and do not be afraid" John 14:27.

God's peace will come as you trade magnifying problems for magnifying Jesus. The joy, peace and love found in His presence will replace your worry and fear. Blessings and joy are available in this life. You don't have to wait until you get to heaven. God wants you to know Him and spend time with Him now. When you walk with Him, you move with Him. Have you given up your own walk to walk with Him?

The Dance

I heard God whisper, "Come dance with me. Let me be your leading man." According to the dictionary, dance is a series of rhythmic and patterned bodily movements usually performed to music. It is an art form. To me, it is also a wonderful reflection of our walk with the Lord.

I think of dancing with a partner as moving in unison, moving as one. My goal is to come to that place where I am moving in unison with the Lord, moving as one with Him. Do you want to know how close God really is? Look at two partners slow dancing. Notice how close they are moving together. He desires to be that near to you.

To start the dance, the man normally begins by moving forward and the woman moves backward. When we move backward we can't see what is behind us. Does the dancer move with fear and panic because she doesn't know what's coming up, fearful she might run into something she can't see? Actually, she is completely relaxed in her partner's arms, trusting him to guide her safely. Just as a partner is trusted to lead in dance, we need to trust God to lead us. This will release us from being fearful of what is ahead. God is saying, "Let go of your fears, let go of your doubts; trust in me. I will guide you."

As soon as the leading man starts moving, his partner moves with him. How did his partner know to move, where to move, how to move? There is a simple answer. It is typical for the man to lead in dance. The woman focuses on the man, watching, sensing and feeling the slightest movement. This gives her the ability to move with him in perfect unison. He guides and leads her with the slightest pressure of his hands and movement of his body. Are you watching, sensing, feeling the slightest movement of God—the Holy Spirit within you—causing you to move effortlessly in unison with Him?

Most of the time, the man's leading in dance isn't seen taking place, yet the partner moves easily. It is not necessary for him to yank or throw his partner around to get her to move in the direction he wants to go. He doesn't run into or over his partner. God doesn't want to do this either to get your attention. As you begin to sense the moving of God, move easily with Him in perfect unison.

Let's break this process down even more. Before the dance begins, a couple has to be aware that the man starts with his left foot and the woman starts with her right foot. They have to know who will do the leading. Therefore, they need some knowledge. In the same way, if you want to move with God, you need some knowledge. We gain understanding and become familiar with His ways and His thoughts by reading and hearing His Word.

Preparation is needed to begin the dance. Since the woman knows she will be moving her right foot first, she stands with the weight of her body on her left foot, leaving her right foot free to move the instant she is led to move. Preparation is also needed to move with God. Time spent in prayer becomes valuable training. You learn to discern His voice and become familiar with the feel of His presence. Then, when you feel His movement or hear the whisper of His voice, you can follow instantly.

The Lord is saying, "Come and dance with me. Focus on me. Move with Me. I am your leading man." Is He your leading man? Is Jesus your Lord and Savior? Do you move in unison with Him?

Finding Freedom

At one time or another, everyone faces a problem of some kind. A person may live with a problem, is working on a problem or makes problems. Many ask how to stop the frustration and pain in their lives? God has not been lax in making it clear that He hates sin, abuse, violence and every evil deed. He will not put up with this kind of behavior forever. A time of judgment will come. For us now, forgiveness is the surgical procedure that releases us from the offender. Forgiving is an ongoing response, a process we continue to walk through. It is possible to forgive the person without condoning the wrongful act.

Forgiving takes away the offending person's power over you; you no longer need to define yourself as that person's victim. It is time to be free from the hurts of the past. When those nasty memories sneak up unexpectedly and no longer bring the pain with them, then you know you are free. Peace at last!

Are you thinking, "This won't work for me; this writer doesn't know what I have been through"? It is true, I don't know what you have been through, but God does. Only He can really understand. Even when you try to explain or describe what you have been through, your listener may grimace or feel compassion for you, but unless they lived through the same situation, they will not truly understand the feelings of deep hurt, sadness, disappointment or grief you have experienced. Proverbs 14:10 says, "Each heart knows its own bitterness, and no one else can share its joy."

Of course, it was wrong for you to be treated badly. Some things should never happen. You didn't deserve it. God didn't plan it for your life. Continuing to harbor those memories only hurts you. By now, the offending person could have forgotten what he did, twisted the truth or lied about it. Maybe he never even cared what he did. In reality, that particular situation no longer exits. It is not part of your life now, so be careful not to live as if it was.

Life is not pleasant when filled with the weeds of resentment and bitterness. It is not worth the effort it takes to harbor unforgiveness. God has provided for your peace. He is ready, willing and able to take your pain away. Each time those old feelings crop up; take them to the Lord immediately. Don't waste time watering negative memories and thoughts anymore. "Cast your cares on the LORD and he will sustain you; he will never let the righteous be shaken" Psalm 55:22.

If you have a need, receive His healing power to mend your pain and emotions. He is able. He is your deliverer and your healer. I'm so glad He is in the healing business, aren't you? Take a moment and be still before Him. Feel His peace. Feel His love.

You will never face anything bigger than God, so make sure to run to the One who can help you and not from Him. He has called you to a higher purpose—one that is ahead of you, not behind you. He can strengthen you and give you hope for the future: "May the God of hope fill you with all joy and peace as you trust in him, so that you may overflow with hope by the power of the Holy Spirit" Romans 15:13. He is always with you. It is possible for you to stray from Him at times, but He will not stray from you. Hold His hand; He will not let go.

Sometimes it takes moving forward with little steps, just one day at a time. Each morning ask God to help you be in control, not your past. Ask Him for His best and for His will to be done in your life. Every night thank Him for walking through the day with you. Psalm 37:23-24 says, "The LORD makes firm the steps of the one who delights in him; though he may stumble, he will not fall, for the LORD upholds him with his hand."

A Wise God

> "Get rid of all bitterness, rage and anger, brawling and slander, along with every form of malice. Be kind and compassion to one another, forgiving each other, just as in Christ God forgave you." Ephesians 4:31-32

We often hear, read or learn so many great truths from God's Word. However, all too frequently those things settle in our minds and do not drop the whole way down into the depths of our hearts. Even though I began to practice forgiving, I soon was full of resentment and bitterness again. I continually recalled one offense after another. To say the words, "I forgive," didn't make the feelings go away. I would cry out to God, "Help me forgive." I would say the words and think it was done. Then later, those old feelings would return. Where was that inner peace I so wanted? I would say the words, "I forgive," but the knot and the tension would still control my body—the offense would still control my mind. Why was this continuing to happen? I had to learn to *continually* release my hurts to God. The action of forgiving had to become a common response in my heart.

The article "Tips to Boost Your Emotional Health" states, "Researchers believe harboring vengeful and painful feelings places your body under continuous stress. In addition to harming your emotional health, holding on to anger may increase your risk of high blood pressure and heart disease."[1]

The *Mayo Clinic Health Letter* article, "Forgiveness and Health" states, "Beyond the hurt of the situation itself, harboring negative feelings and thoughts may influence your psychological and even physical health. Research indicates that learning to forgive and move on is a better choice for overall health."[2]

It is a medical fact that how we think or feel can affect the health of our bodies. In fact, the Bible agrees that it is possible for emotions to affect our bodies. For instance, in Proverbs 15:13, we read, "A happy heart makes the face cheerful, but heartache crushes the spirit." Other Scriptures tell us:

> "A heart at peace gives life to the body, but envy rots the bones." Proverbs 14:30

> "A cheerful heart is good medicine, but a broken spirit saps a person's strength." Proverbs 17:22 (NLT)

> "Hope deferred makes the heart sick; but when dreams come true at last, there is life and joy." Proverbs 13:12 (TLB)

By the miserable state I was in, I could see that embracing offenses was hurting me more than the one I couldn't forgive. What I failed to understand was that by forgiving others, I give God the opportunity to work in their lives. We are actually releasing them and that situation into the hands of our heavenly Father. As I searched the Scriptures on forgiveness, I found a verse in the section referred to as the Lord's Prayer that reads, "And forgive us our debts, as we also have forgiven our debtors" Matthew 6:12. In this passage, the word *debt* refers to moral debts or sins.

Unforgiveness results in resentment, anger and bitterness, which only compounds our stress. Forgiving others is really for our sake, as we have read. Otherwise, our mental, emotional and physical health can be adversely affected. We have a very wise God; He knows what He is talking about when He tells us to forgive. Why continue to carry that weight on our shoulders when we don't have to? God was willing to forgive us. If we are to follow His example, then we must forgive others. Dr. Asa Andrew wrote:

> "Our ability to forgive others when they have hurt us is a secret to achieving the optimal health that God has for us. One of the hardest areas of emotional health is forgiveness....

> Research shows us that just one moment of anger will compromise the immune system for up to eight hours....Your health depends on your ability to forgive."[3]

If we don't forgive we are actually making ourselves that person's judge, but Jesus is our ultimate judge. A person may sin on purpose or unknowingly because of deception. Since God weighs the motives of the heart, He is able to judge righteously. It is not our responsibility but His. When others act irresponsibly and hurt us, they have to settle their sins, wrongdoings and their own hurt and pain with the Lord, just as we do.

What was most helpful to me was realizing how much God loved me. Jesus was willing to die for me before I ever asked Him to forgive me, and He still loved me if I made mistakes or had setbacks. "If we confess our sins, he is faithful and just and will forgive us our sins and purify us from all unrighteousness" 1 John 1:9.

There is also the matter of forgiving yourself. Do you keep recalling those things you should have done but didn't do? Do you keep recalling those things that you did that you wish you had not done? If feelings of guilt or condemnation keep you going around in circles, it may be necessary to forgive yourself. God is willing to forgive you, so forgive yourself too. Say goodbye to guilt.

God sent His son Jesus to be our substitute and pay the penalty for our sins. "This is how we know what love is: Jesus Christ laid down his life for us" 1 John 3:16. Jesus is our Savior. Now we have the opportunity to stand before Him cleansed from sin and accepted. Forgiveness is real and God is serious about it. Jesus paid a high price because of it.

"Therefore, there is now no condemnation for those who are in Christ Jesus" Romans 8:1.

The blood of Jesus removed the need for a guilty conscious, when you accepted the sin payment He made for you. Now conviction of a wrong will bring hope instead of guilt. Realize that as perfect and as right as you want to be, you are still human. Now and then mistakes are made or a weakness prevails. There is no need to punish yourself for something God forgave long ago. He forgave you the moment His Son died on the cross. When you accepted Jesus as your Savior, that forgiveness was applied to your life.

While in this world, take the time to become acquainted with the God who loves you. He desires and expects you to spend eternity with Him. Strive to become more and more like His Son. Jesus freed you to live a godly life by removing the power that sin had over you. The Holy Spirit came to move in with you, and He empowers you to live that godly life. God cares more about what you become than in what you have done. Who can know what amazing things will be accomplished as you face the future with Him.

The things that happened in the past were a part of your life. It is OK to acknowledge the pain they may have caused you. Then it is time to have a memorial service and put them to rest. Commit to forgiveness so you can heal—it is God's way. Being forgiven by God and forgiving others, bring the awesome side effects of harmony and peacefulness. Author and speaker Gary Chapman said, "Love doesn't erase the past, but it makes the future different."

God wants the best for you. The Lord is the One who brings true healing, not just a bandage. He is the One who brings true forgiveness, not just a rash word. He reaches into the souls of men because He created them. He has so much love for you. Know Him as the Father who loves you and heals you.

On to Victory

> "Now may the Lord of peace himself give you peace at all times and in every way."
> 2 Thessalonians 3:16

I have concluded that life is a series of surprises and challenges. Often times, it wasn't quite what I expected or the way I wanted it to be. But the most important thing for me was loving and trusting the Lord with all my heart through it all. He gave me the strength to endure and conquer the trials of life—even when I thought I couldn't, because He can! To all His lonely ones and lost ones who are hurting, come to know the Lord and see Him in a different light. He is not far away. He isn't unreachable. He is close by and your prayers reach His ears. He is God of the universe; watch what He can do.

Our faith turns us to God. Even though this life is tough at times, it is temporary. We look forward to eternity in His love and presence. God has a plan for each of us. He gives us hope and a future. We have to look where we are going, not only where we have been. As believers in the Son of God, the Holy Spirit gives us strength to overcome, to have victory over the sinful pattern of this world.

He wants to share with us all that is His, just as we share with our children what is ours. Paul said it this way, "Now if we are children, then we are heirs—heirs of God and co-heirs with Christ" Romans 8:17. Even though some people think He is waiting to send hardship and sickness their way, or waiting with a whip just to catch them in the slightest sin or mistake, this is not true. As believers in Jesus, God calls us His children. It was because of His love for us that He willingly sacrificed His son to re-establish a relationship with us by providing the way for our sins to be forgiven.

He gave us the Holy Spirit, who teaches, corrects, guides and directs us. The Bible, His Word, teaches us how to live, how to love each other and how to love Him. It shows us how to avoid sin and the consequences it brings, although experience is oftentimes its own teacher. The nature of sin destroys, but God's mercy and grace saves us. He enhances our lives with blessings and His promises.

He wants you to know Him and experience His presence. When you encounter trouble, you can run to Him. He is there to help you through it or out of it. He is a restoring God. His love for you is awesome! When there is no way out, let God in. If you feel weak or overwhelmed, God will give you the extra strength you need to carry on. Answers or solutions may come to mind. As you stay focused on Him, watch your problems lessen, become less significant, or simply fade away.

> *When there is no way out, let God in.*

Going through the storms of life with God may not always eliminate the problem, but the worry and fear will be replaced with joy and peace. Sometimes it is your reaction that changes, not just the circumstances. He is your helper, your strength and your future. Suffering takes its toll, but healing comes in time. So, do not give up and do not give in.

The evil one looks around to see whom he can overtake. He doesn't give up easily, so stick close to the Lord. It doesn't matter if events go the way we expect them to or not; we can learn from both the good and bad times. It doesn't matter if you're having a super day or a miserable day; God is still with you. Look up instead of down, not losing sight of the bigger picture. Even though the journey is hard at times, continue to move forward with confidence in God. There is safety and protection in His presence: "How priceless is your unfailing love, O God! People take refuge in the shadow of your wings" Psalm 36:7.

Do you tend to stress over every little thing? Many things can weigh on your heart and mind. One time the Lord told me, "At times life is not as difficult as you make it. Put aside the struggles and listen to my heart; it beats for you." And I want you to know, His heart beats for you too. To reject or deny God takes the hope out of life. Even though you don't understand all things, you can trust Him in all things.

Paul wrote, "So we do not look at what we can see right now, the troubles all around us, but we look forward to the joys in heaven which we have not yet seen. The troubles will soon be over, but the joys to come will last forever" 2 Corinthians 4:18 (TLB). The future is our hope. Troubles and struggles are temporary; eternity waits behind the scenes. Jesus "died for us so that we can live with him forever" 1 Thessalonians 5:10 (TLB). So let's smile, be the light and dance for the Lord.

He encourages you saying,

"Go, and I will go with you.
Be, and I will be with you.
Do, and I will do it with you."

In other words, He means, "*We* will." The Lord said to Paul, "My grace is sufficient for you, for my power is made perfect in weakness." 2 Corinthians 12:9. God is here; He is with you. That is all you really need. His power shows up best through your weaknesses. Instead of depending on your own power and abilities, you can be a living demonstration of His power.

From time to time, rest in Him and enjoy watching Him work for you. All power is in His hands; there is nothing impossible for Him. Are you living with His presence in mind? Live from this point, understanding His character and all that He can do.

The trials of life don't have to beat you down. Stand tall. Stand strong. Your problems are small in comparison to God's greatness. See them through His eyes and your confidence in Him will grow bigger than any problem you face. With Jesus, you come out on top. You are the victor, not the victim. Paul wrote, "In these things we are more than conquerors through him who loved us" Romans 8:37.

His love will sustain you. His love is all encompassing. All else is a bonus, a blessing. When you walk in His light, on His path of love and forgiveness, you will find the contentment, joy and peace you crave—peace in your heart, in your mind and in your soul. Do you hear the Lord saying:

> "I hide in the secret places and wait for you to come to me. I am your God, but I am also your father and your friend. I am whatever you need me to be. So come to me. Don't turn away from me, no matter what this life throws at you, for the best is yet to come and comes through me.

Rejoice in my presence for I love you so. Believe me when I tell you. Come away with me to that secret place where you and I will commune. Dance before me and leap for joy. In my presence, love abounds.

Like rays of the sun that radiate across the sky—shining through the clouds until they touch the earth, like the rays of sun that dart across the water—glittering like diamonds along its path, so I come to touch you and light up your life. Hold unto me as a child holds his parent's hand and I will lead you and guide you to only places I can take you."

"The LORD gives victory to his anointed.
He answers him from his heavenly sanctuary
with the victorious power of his right hand.
Some trust in chariots and some in horses,
but we trust in the name of the LORD our God."
Psalm 20:6-7

End Notes

Chapter 1
What to Do?

Too Much Worry

1. WebMD, "Anxiety – Topic Overview," http://www.webmd.com/anxiety-panic/tc/anxiety-topic-overview.

Moving Forward

2. Robert J. Hastings essay, "The Station."

Chapter 6
A Pity Party

A Pity Party

1. Dale Flynn, *Word of Life Extended Ministries to Churches (EMC),* newsletter, December 2012.

Chapter 7
Wounds of the Heart

Wounds of the Heart

1. Dr. Henry Cloud and Dr. John Townsend, *Safe People* (Grand Rapids, Michigan: Zondervan, 1995), 193.

He was There

2. Becky Hunter, "Becky Hunter's Random Bits of Wisdom," January 7, 2013, http://www.northland-church.net/blogs/category/beckyhunter/.

Stressing Out

3. PJ, "Thought For The Day," August 20, 2014, http://www.signs-and-wonders.org

Chapter 8
Bemoaning the Times

Bemoaning the Times

1. Carolyn Shockey, "Your Legacy," *Senior Voice America, Inc.* August 2014, Page 21, P.O. Box 1379, Lutz, FL 33548-1379

Chapter 11
New Memories

Rehashing the Past

1. Gary Chapman, *The 5 Love Languages* (Chicago, IL: Northfield Publishing, 2010), 44.

Upsetting Thoughts

2. Krissy Brady, "A Surprisingly Easy Way to Stop Reliving Embarrassing Moments," May 22, 2014, http://www.doctoroz.com/videos/surprisingly-easy-way-stop-reliving-embarrassing-moments

Another Perspective

3. Medad Birungi with Craig Borlase, *Tombstones and Banana Trees* (Colorado Springs, CO: David C Cook, 2011), 153.

Chapter 12
The Blessing of Peace

A Wise God

1. "Tips to Boost Your Emotional Health," *Just for the Health of It,* a News Leader Publication, February 2003
2. "Forgiveness and Health," *Mayo Clinic Health Letter*, December 2005

3. Dr. Asa Andrew, "A Weekly e-House Call," *The Health Prescription,* Issue 120, September 13, 2006, www.drasa.com

Further Reading

Thom Gardner, *Healing the Wounded Heart*. Shippensburg, PA: Destiny Image Publishers, Inc., 2005.

Thom Gardner, *the Healing Journey*. Shippensburg, PA: Destiny Image Publishers, Inc., 2010.

John F. Westfall, *Getting Past What You'll Never Get Over*. Grand Rapids, MI: Revell, a division of Baker Publishing Group.

Medad Birungi with Craig Borlase, *Tombstones and Banana Trees,* Colorado Springs, CO: David C Cook, 2011.

Dr. Henry Cloud and Dr. John Townsend, *Safe People*. Grand Rapids, MI: Zondervan, 1995.

Dr. Henry Cloud and Dr. John Townsend, *Boundaries*. Grand Rapids, MI: Zondervan, 1992.

Gary Chapman, *The 5 Love Languages*. Chicago, IL: Northfield Publishing, 2010.

About the Author

Author and writer, Nancy L. Harry, founded Eagles Rest, Dunedin, Florida to promote God's love and Word. Her mission is three-fold: to carry the message of God's love and the impact it has on our daily lives, to prepare us for Christ's return and to offer helpful suggestions as we make our way over the bumps in the road of life. With Scripture and experiences from her own Christian walk, she encourages others as they continue in their walk with the Lord.

Nancy is a graduate of the ORU Ministry Training and Development Institute. She has been active in local and international ministries, holding positions as a local board member for Aglow International and as a speaker for Stonecroft Ministries.

She spends her time writing and basking in the warmth of the Florida sunshine. Her heart's desire is to see healing—physically, emotionally and spiritually—manifested in the body of Christ. Her prayer is for all to be rooted in love, and have the power to understand and know Christ's deep love.

www.e-eaglesrest.com

CPSIA information can be obtained at www.ICGtesting.com
Printed in the USA
LVOW06s2203090915

453559LV00012B/142/P